Betty Joyce Metheny
Drago Niels ~ England
October 1990

TRADITIONAL
NURSERY PATTERNS

JUDITH HOPKINSON

BLOOMSBURY

First published 1988
Bloomsbury Publishing Limited
2 Soho Square
London W1V 5DE

*Designed and produced by Rosemary Wilkinson
and Malcolm Saunders Publishing Ltd
26 Ornan Road
London NW3 4QB*

Editor: *Rosemary Wilkinson*
Illustrators: *Elsa Godfrey*
Judith Hopkinson
Photographers: *Guglielmo Galvin*
George Taylor

British Library Cataloguing in Publication Data
Hopkinson, Judith
Traditional nursery patterns.
1. Babies' clothing. Making – Patterns
I. Title
646.4'09

ISBN 0–7475–0223–4

**Typeset by Fakenham Photosetting Ltd
Printed in Spain**

Front cover: Smocked dress for a 12 month old girl and
buster suit for an 18 month old boy.
With thanks to Galt Toys.

CONTENTS

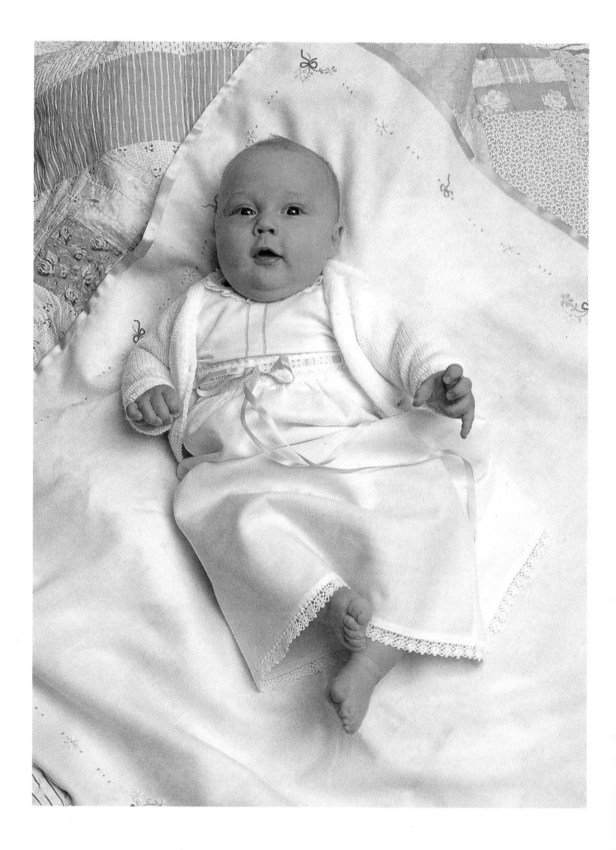

INTRODUCTION

Before the First World War, babies and children were strictly confined to the nursery under the care of 'Nanny' and were allowed to visit their parents only at stated times. Fortunately, parents today are much more involved in caring for their children but, as many mothers wish for the freedom to carry on with their careers, good nannies are still in great demand.

Top nannies like their charges to be nicely turned out and will dress them in traditional clothes: smocked dresses for girls, buster and romper suits for boys and nightgowns for babies. Parties are occasions when Nannies and mothers alike wish to show off. Nanny will dress her charges in the same traditional style as they wear for everyday activities but she will choose finer materials, such as organdie, voile, silk – and for colder weather – veruna wool. Mothers who dress their children more casually during a normal day still turn to these classic styles for special occasions.

Ancient rules of thumb about which clothes should be worn, at what age, on what occasion and which colours should be chosen are rapidly falling by the wayside. However, there are some un-written rules still adhered to, handed down from Nanny to Nanny, and I have included a few of these amongst this collection of traditional children's patterns. These cover both the classic clothes themselves and the smaller accessories worn with them, such as the socks and shoes.

With a little care and attention, dressmaking and knitting are easy and inexpensive ways of obtaining these classic clothes, many of which are now hard to find elsewhere. Simplicity is the keynote of traditional babies' clothes, with the plainness of the white or cream material being relieved by cleverly matched trimmings, embroidery, smocking and/or ribbons. Clothes for toddlers may also be trimmed with material in a contrasting colour.

The choice of materials is all-important in making these clothes look professional and I have given guidance on this in a separate section. Pastel shades were thought to be the most becoming for babies. I have kept to these in my selection of materials, only introducing brighter colours in the last sections for children aged 18 months and over. The modern mother may, however, prefer to substitute primary-coloured materials to make these projects in, and the garments will be admired just as much as those in the more traditional colourways.

No baby's wardrobe is complete without knitted garments and, although these may be bought, hand knitting remains a firm favourite, particularly as a present from relatives and friends to the newborn baby. The patterns in this book have been developed using mainly two and three ply yarns, which give a delicate look to the finished garment. Within each section they have been designed with embroidery, lace and/or ribbons to match or tone with the dresses and romper suits.

It is worth bearing in mind the various ways of extending the life of the clothes, perhaps making them slightly too large, turning up a deep hemline, or adding an extra tuck. It makes sense to buy good quality materials, which will stand up to the wear and washing that children engender, so that long after the garment has been outgrown by one child, it can be passed on to brothers or sisters, or stored for future generations.

To this end I have included instructions for storage of these garments in the techniques section at the back of the book, which also contains fully illustrated and detailed descriptions of the traditional knitting, sewing and embroidery methods used to make these nursery clothes.

ABBREVIATIONS

k	*knit*
p	*purl*
st(s)	*stitch(es)*
tog.	*together*
k2tog	*knit two stitches together*
p2tog	*purl two stitches together*
inc.	*increase*
dec.	*decrease*
yfwd	*yarn forward*
yrn	*yarn round needle*
rep.	*repeat*
sl.1	*slip one stitch*
st. st	*stocking stitch*
psso	*pass slipped stitch over*
alt.	*alternate*
tbl	*through back of loop*
in	*inch*
mm	*millimetre*
cm	*centimetre*

KNITTING NEEDLE SIZES

English	Metric	American
5	5½ mm	8
6	5 mm	7
7	4½ mm	6
8	4 mm	5
9	3¾ mm	4
10	3¼ mm	3
11	3 mm	2
12	2¾ mm	1
13	2¼ mm	0

NOTES

1. Unless otherwise stated the seam allowance is 1 cm (⅜ in) throughout the sewing patterns.
2. Work with either metric or imperial measurements but do not mix them within one pattern as they are not exact equivalents.

WOOL/TENSION

Specific wool brands have not been named in the list of materials needed. Provided a good quality yarn is chosen (see page 121), of the correct ply, the difference in the end result on such small garments will not be significant. For the same reason, no instructions for the tension have been given.

BASIC TECHNIQUES

The section beginning on page 100 gives detailed instructions on all the knitting, sewing and embroidery techniques used in making the garments. Also contained here are invaluable hints on choosing the correct materials, as well as details on how to look after the garments once completed.

Check this section if you are unsure of any procedure in the pattern instructions.

NEWBORN

Nightgown for a newborn baby (see page 14) with matching cardigan and bootees (pages 16 and 18) together with the nestling blanket, trimmed in matching colours (page 20)

NEWBORN

Nanny will keep a young baby in a nightgown, rather than a dress, during the day, until he is 'shortened' at 3 to 4 months. These nightgowns are always white or cream; colour at this age being introduced only by embroidery and/or coloured ribbons and edgings.

A cardigan and bootees are worn, both trimmed to match the nightgown and would be knitted in either white or cream, again depending on the colour of the nightgown. The lace edging on the sleeve of the nightgown will be pulled down around the wrist to show below the sleeve of the cardigan. Traditionally Nanny will often knit two pairs of bootees for every cardigan, so that a non-matching pair need never be worn, should the bootees become dirty before the cardigan.

A baby likes to feel secure and, even indoors, Nanny wraps him in a nestling blanket to sleep, which is trimmed with the same colour as the clothes he is wearing that day. The nestling blanket is used until baby is six to eight weeks old but Nanny finds it invaluable for other purposes after that, for instance, as a loose indoor shawl, across baby's lap instead of a rug when he is sitting in his bouncing chair or car seat, as an attractive crib or pram sheet, or to cover the floor, making a clean area for baby to lie and play.

The nightgown and nestling blanket shown in the photograph on page 12 are made from Viyella, a wool and cotton mixture traditionally associated with children's wear. It is soft but wears well, even with the constant washing which a baby creates.

The matching cardigan and bootees are knitted in 2 ply, as a thick wool so easily looks bulky on such a tiny baby. The first cardigan pattern is a size which will only fit in baby's first few weeks but it is nice to have at least one cardigan which does not swamp him. The second cardigan (a V-neck pattern shown on page 8) may be worn by a newborn baby but will fit best from approximately six weeks. Swiss darning has been worked on this cardigan to make a flower border round the welt.

NIGHTGOWN

SIZE: NEWBORN

MATERIALS

1 metre (1 yard), white Viyella, Clydella or
similar, 90 cm (36 in) or 115 cm (45 in) wide

1 metre (1 yard), green satin ribbon, 6 mm
(¼ in) wide

1 metre (1 yard), green satin ribbon, 3 mm
(⅛ in) wide

30 cm (12 in), white broderie anglaise eyelet
insertion, 13 mm (½ in) wide

70 cm (28 in), white cotton lace edging, 6 mm
(¼ in) wide

20 cm (8 in), single cord elastic

1 skein, green embroidery silk

THE PATTERN
Enlarge the pattern pieces given on pages 22 and 23. Following the diagrams on page 15, lay and cut out pattern, including a 3 × 30 cm (1¼ × 12 in) bias strip for the binding around the neckline. Mark all dots with tailor's tacks.

WITHDRAWN WORK ON FRONT YOKE
1. Following the instructions on page 115, withdraw 5 threads, 2 cm (¾ in) apart, down the centre

front as marked on the yoke pattern. Using 2 strands of embroidery silk, work ladder hem stitch down the drawn threads.

TO MAKE THE NIGHTGOWN

JOINING THE YOKE AND FRONT SKIRT

2. Make 2 rows of hand or machine gathering stitches between the dots along the top edge of the skirt front, as marked on the pattern. With *wrong* sides together, pin the centre front of the skirt to the centre front of the yoke with raw edges level, pull up the gathers until the skirt fits the yoke. Pin in place, then stitch across the seam. Do not press at this stage.
NB This leaves the raw edge of the seam on the *right* side of the garment.
Remove the gathering threads.

THE BELT

3. With *right* sides of the skirt and belt together, align the stitching line at the bottom edge of the front belt along the waist seam just made, matching the centre of the belt to the centre of the skirt. Pin through all 3 layers and stitch.
4. Fold and press the yoke and the belt away from the skirt. Topstitch along the bottom edge of the belt. Turn under the seam allowance along the top edge of the belt to make the belt 3 cm (1¼ in) wide. Topstitch to the yoke (thus enclosing the seam).
5. Thread 50 cm (½ yard) of 6 mm (¼ in) wide ribbon from each side of broderie anglaise eyelet insertion, leaving excess ribbon hanging from centre. Topstitch the broderie anglaise eyelet insertion across the centre of the belt with the hanging ribbons in the middle.

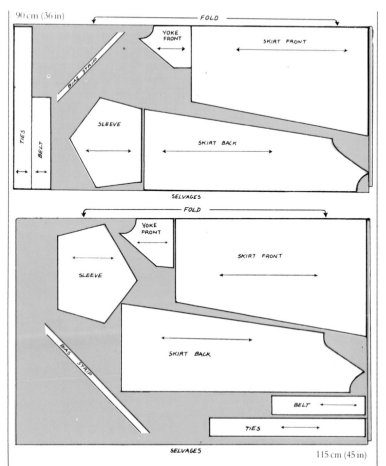

THE TIES

6. Turn a narrow hem down one long side of both ties, machine-stitching in place.
7. Lay ties *right* side up. Fold one end of each piece diagonally to align with unfinished long side (*right* sides together) and pin the 2 raw edges together. Starting at the pointed end, stitch along pinned edge. Turn *right* side out and pin a narrow hem down the unfinished edge, making tie 3 cm (1¼ in) wide. Stitch.
8. With *right* sides together, align the ties against the seams of the belt. Pin and tack in place.

THE BACK

9. Neaten the centre seam edges of the back. With *right* sides together, pin the centre back seam leaving a 16 cm (6¼ in) opening at top. Stitch in place with a plain seam. Press.
10. Join the side seams of the front and back with a french seam.

THE SLEEVES

11. Make a narrow 6 mm (¼ in) casing along the wrist of the sleeve. Stitch a row of lace on *right* side as near to the edge of the casing as possible to overhang the edge of the sleeve. Cut 2 pieces of cord elastic approximately 7 cm (2¾ in) long (adjust here if necessary to size of the baby's wrist plus 2 cm (¾ in)). Thread the elastic through the casing and catch at the sides with a stitch.
12. Join the edges of the sleeve with a french seam (securing

elastic at the same time). Press.
13. With the nightgown inside out and with *right* sides together, align the side seams of the sleeves with the side seam of the dress. Pin as shown in the cutaway diagram. Continue up the edges of the shoulder seams, aligning them with corresponding edges of front and back pieces. Pin in place, tack, then stitch with a plain seam. Trim surplus material at the top of the sleeve.
14. Neaten the edges of the seam.

THE NECKLINE

15. Press under the edges of the centre back opening and make a narrow hem.
16. Attach the bias strip around the neckline, making the finished width 5 mm (³⁄₁₆ in) and leaving

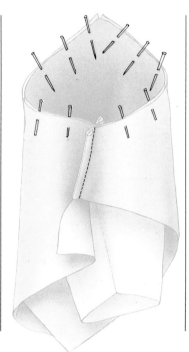

the opening free. Thread 60 cm (24 in) of 3 mm (⅛ in) ribbon through, leaving ends hanging.
17. Gather the remaining lace and stitch around the neckline where the binding joins the yoke.

FINISHING THE NIGHTGOWN

18. Make a narrow 6 mm (¼ in) hem round nightgown bottom.
19. With 2 strands of embroidery silk, feather stitch above and below ribbon insert on the belt. Tie the ribbons in middle of the belt into a bow.
20. Make 2 small bows with the remaining narrow ribbon and stitch in place on the centre edge of both sleeves just above the lace. For alternative embroidery, see page 21.

2 PLY HIGH NECK CARDIGAN

SIZE: NEWBORN
MATERIALS
40 grams (1½ oz) × 2 ply white wool
2 skeins pale green embroidery silk
6 small white buttons
1 pair 2¾ mm (no. 12) needles
medium crochet hook

BACK AND FRONTS
(*knitted in 1 piece up to armholes*)
Cast on 146 sts.
Row 1: ★ k1, p1, repeat from ★ to end.
Row 2: k2, ★ p1, k1, repeat from ★ to last st, k1.
Row 3: k1, p1, k1, yfwd, k2tog, ★ p1, k1, rep. from ★ to last st, k1. Repeat row 2, then repeat rows 1 & 2 four more times to form moss stitch border.
Row 13: moss st 6, knit to last 6 sts, moss st 6.
Row 14 and alt. rows: moss st 6, purl to last 6 sts, moss st 6.
Row 15: k1, p1, k1, yfwd, k2tog, p1, knit to last 6 sts, moss st 6.

Row 17: moss st 6, k5 (yfwd, sl.1, k1, psso, k1, k2tog, yfwd, k2), repeat brackets to last 16 sts, yfwd, sl.1, k1, psso, k1, k2tog, yfwd, k5, moss st 6.
Row 19: moss st 6, k6 (yfwd, sl.1, k2tog, psso, yfwd, k4), repeat brackets to last 15 sts, yfwd, sl.1, k2tog, psso, yfwd, k6, moss st 6.
Row 21: moss st 6, knit to last 6 sts, moss st 6.
Row 23: moss st 6, k5, yfwd, sl.1, k1, psso, k1, k2tog, yfwd, knit to last 16 sts, yfwd, sl.1, k1, psso, k1, k2tog, yfwd, k5, moss st 6.
Row 25: moss st 6, k6, yfwd,

sl.1, k2tog, psso, yfwd, knit to last 15 sts, yfwd, sl.1, k2tog, psso, yfwd, k6, moss st 6.
Row 26: moss st 6, purl to last 6 sts, moss st 6.
The 6 rows (21 to 26) form the pattern.
Keeping buttonband and border pattern correct, st. st 16 rows working a buttonhole on the 3rd row, and ending with a purl row.

ARMHOLES
Keeping border pattern correct:
Next row: k1, p1, k1, yfwd, k2tog, p1, work 28 sts, cast off 10 sts, knit until there are 58 sts on right-hand needle after cast off sts,

cast off next 10 sts, work to last 6 sts, moss st 6.
(This should give 34 sts for the right front, 58 sts for the back and 34 sts for the left front.)
Turn and work on the first 34 sts for the left front, still keeping the border pattern correct.
Row 1: moss st 6, purl to end.
Row 2: k1, sl.1, k1, psso, knit and pattern to last 6 sts, moss st 6.
Repeat last 2 rows until 24 sts remain, ending with a dec. row.

SHAPING NECK
Moss st 6, p4, slip these 10 sts on to a safety-pin for the neckband, purl to end. Continue to dec. on alt. rows at raglan edge as before. *At the same time* dec. 1 st at the neck edge on next 3 rows.
Discontinue lace pattern at neck edge where necessary.
Dec. 1 st at neck and raglan edges on every alt. row until there are 5 sts left, ending with a purl row.
Next row: k1, sl.1, k2tog, psso, k1.
Next row: purl 3 sts.
Next row: k1, k2tog.
Next row: purl 2 sts.
Next row: k2tog, and fasten off.
With wrong side of work facing, rejoin yarn to next st and purl 58 sts, for the back.
Next row: k1, sl.1, k1, psso, knit to last 3 sts, k2tog, k1.
Next row: purl.
Repeat last 2 rows until 32 sts remain ending with a purl row.
Next row: k1, sl.1, k2tog, psso, knit to last 4 sts, k3tog, k1.
Next row: purl.
Repeat last 2 rows once. Leave remaining 24 sts on a safety-pin.
With wrong side of work facing, rejoin yarn to next st and purl to last 6 sts, moss st 6.
Continue, keeping border pattern correct:
Next row: moss st 6, work to last 3 sts, k2tog, k1.
Next row: purl to last 6 sts, moss st 6.

Repeat last 2 rows until 24 sts remain, working a buttonhole on 11th row, ending with a purl row.

SHAPING NECK
Moss st 6, k4, slip these 10 sts on to a safety-pin for the neckband, knit to last 3 sts, k2tog, k1.
Continue to dec. at the raglan edge on every alt. row as before, *at the same time* dec. 1 st at neck edge on next 2 rows. Discontinue the lace pattern where necessary at neck edge as on left front.
Dec. 1 st at neck and raglan edge on every alt. row until 5 sts remain, ending with a purl row.
Next row: k1, sl.1, k2tog, psso, k1.
Next row: purl 3 sts.
Next row: k2tog, k1.
Next row: purl 2 sts.
Next row: k2tog, and fasten off.

SLEEVES
Cast on 43 sts.
Moss st 10 rows.
Next row: stocking st 4 rows.
Inc. 1 st at each end of next and every following 5th row until 55 sts remain.
Continue in st. st on these sts for 12 rows, ending with a purl row.
Cast off 5 sts at beginning of next 2 rows.
Next row: k1, sl.1, k1, psso, knit to last 3 sts, k2tog, k1.
Next row: purl.
Repeat last 2 rows until 19 sts remain, ending with a purl row.
Next row: k1, sl.1, k2tog, psso, knit to last 4 sts, k3tog, k1.
Next row: purl.
Repeat last 2 rows until 7 sts remain and leave on a safety-pin for the neckband.

NECKBAND
Slip first 6 sts of right front buttonband from safety-pin on to needle and knit across remaining 4 sts on safety-pin. Continuing on, pick up and knit 11 sts up right front neck slope, knit across 7 sts

from one sleeve, 24 sts from back and 7 sts from second sleeve. Pick up and knit 11 sts down left front slope, knit across first 4 sts from remaining safety-pin, then moss st 6 sts of buttonband. (80 sts.)
Moss st 3 rows on these stitches.
Next row: moss st 3, yfwd, k2tog, moss st to end.
Moss st 2 rows.
Cast off in moss st.

TO MAKE UP
Sew together the raglan seams, then the sleeve seams.
Sew the buttons on to the buttonband in corresponding place to buttonholes.
Using the crochet hook and 6 strands of pale green embroidery silk, chain stitch into each stitch beginning centre back (see diagram below), around the edge of the moss stitch border, up the buttonband, round the neckband, down the buttonhole band and along the edge of the moss stitch border to the centre back. Tie off.
Sew the loose ends in.
Using 3 strands of pale green embroidery silk, make french knots in the centre of each inverted V in the border pattern.

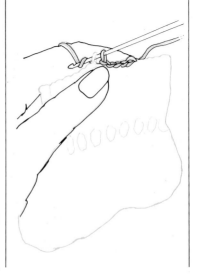

BOOTEES
SIZE: NEWBORN
MATERIALS
20 grams (1 oz) × 2 ply, white wool
1 metre (1 yard) white satin ribbon, 6 mm (¼ in) wide
scrap of pale green embroidery silk
1 pair 3 mm (no. 11) needles

Cast on 45 sts.
Knit 2 rows.
Row 1: k1, * inc. 1 st, k19, inc. 1 st, k1, repeat from * to end of row.
Row 2 and all alt. rows: knit.
Row 3: k1, (inc. 1 st, k20, inc. 1 st), k3, repeat bracket once, k1.
Row 5: k1, (inc. 1 st, k21, inc. 1 st), k5, repeat bracket once, k1.
Row 7: k1, (inc. 1 st, k22, inc. 1 st), k7, repeat bracket once, k1.
Knit 3 rows.
Purl 1 row.
Knit 3 rows.
Next row: * k1, p1, repeat from * to end of row.
Repeat last row twice.

Knit 2 rows.

SHAPING FOOT
Row 1: k36, k2tog tb1, turn,
Row 2: slip 1 purlwise, p11, p2tog, turn,
Row 3: slip 1, k11, k2tog tb1, turn,
Repeat rows 2 and 3 seven times, then row 2 once.
Next row: knit to end. (43 sts.)
Next row: inc. 1 st in first st, * p1, k1, repeat from * to end of row.
Next row: k2, * yfwd, k2tog, repeat from * to end of row.
Next row: k2tog, * p1, k1, repeat from * to end of row.

Next row: k1, k2tog, k17, k2tog, k18, k2tog, k1. (40 sts.)
Moss st 14 rows.
Cast off loosely.

TO MAKE UP
Using 3 strands of embroidery silk, sew french knots around the shaped top of foot, approximately 1 cm (⅜ in) apart. Sew together the sole, then the back seam. Using a crochet hook and embroidery silk, chain stitch into each stitch of cast-off edge, see diagram page 17. Tie off. Sew the loose ends in.
Cut the white satin ribbon in half and thread through the eyelets.

3 PLY CARDIGAN
SIZE: 6 WEEKS
MATERIALS
40 grams (2 oz) × 3 ply, white wool
scraps of embroidery silk in pastel shades
4 small white buttons with star-shaped cut-out
1 pair each 3¼ mm & 2¾ mm (nos. 10 & 12) needles

BACK
Using 2¾ mm (no. 12) needles, cast on 61 sts.
Rib 10 rows.
Change to 3¼ mm (no. 10) needles.
Stocking st 30 rows, ending with a purl row.
Cast off 3 sts at the beginning of next 2 rows.
Next row: k1, sl.1, k1, psso, knit to last 3 sts, k2tog, k1.
Next row: k1, purl to last st, k1.
Repeat last 2 rows until 25 sts remain on needle.
Cast off.

RIGHT FRONT
Using 2¾ mm (no. 12) needles, cast on 35 sts. (This includes 6 sts for the border.)
Rib 2 rows, beginning k2, p1, k1,

p1, . . .
Next row: make buttonhole as follows: k2, p1, yfwd, k2tog, rib to end.
Rib 7 more rows.
Change to 3¼ mm (no. 10) needles and work in stocking st with rib border:
Next row: k2, p1, k1, p1, knit to end.
Next row: k1, purl to last 6 sts,

rib to end.

Continue for 29 more rows, working buttonholes on rows 3, 15 and 27 and ending with a knit row.

Next row: cast off 3 sts, purl to last 8 sts, p2tog, rib 6.

Next row: rib 6, knit to last 3 sts, k2tog, k1.

Next row: k1, purl to last 6 sts, rib 6.

Next row: rib 6, knit to last 3 sts, k2tog, k1.

Next row: k1, purl to last 8 sts, p2tog, rib 6.

Repeat last 4 rows until 13 sts remain.

Decrease at raglan only until 10 sts remain.

Next row: k1, p3, rib 6.

Next row: rib 6, k1, k2tog, k1.

Next row: k1, p2, rib 6.

Next row: rib 6, k2tog, k1.

Next row: k1, p1, rib 6.

Next row: rib 5, k3tog.

Rib 18 more rows on these 6 sts. Cast off.

LEFT FRONT

Using 2¾ mm (no. 12) needles, cast on 35 sts. (This includes 6 sts for the border.)

Rib 10 rows, starting k2, p1, k1, p1, . . .

Change to 3¼ mm (no. 10) needles and work in stocking st with rib border:

Next row: knit to last 6 sts, rib 6.

Next row: rib 6, purl to last st, k1.

Continue for 28 more rows, ending with a purl row.

Next row: cast off 3 sts, knit to last 8 sts, k2tog, rib 6.

Next row: rib 6, purl to last st, k1.

Next row: k1, sl.1, k1, psso, knit to last 6 sts, rib 6.

Next row: rib 6, purl to last st, k1.

Next row: k1, sl.1, k1, psso, knit to last 8 sts, k2tog, rib 6.

Repeat last 4 rows until 13 sts remain.

Decrease at raglan edge only until 10 sts remain.

Next row: rib 6, p3, k1.

Next row: k1, sl.1, k1, psso, k1, rib 6.

Next row: rib 6, p2, k1.

Next row: k1, sl.1, k1, psso, rib 6.

Next row: rib 6, p1, k1.

Next row: k3tog, rib 5.

Rib 18 more rows on these 6 sts. Cast off.

SLEEVES

Using 2¾ mm (no. 12) needles, cast on 33 sts.

Rib 8 rows.

Change to 3¼ mm (no. 10) needles and stocking st 6 rows.

Continue in stocking st, increasing 1 st at each end of next and every 4th row until 47 sts. Work 9 rows without shaping. Cast off 3 sts at beginning of next 2 rows.

Next row: k1, sl.1, k1, psso, knit to last 3 sts, k2tog, k1.

Next row: k1, purl to last st, k1.

Repeat last 2 rows until 7 sts remain.

Cast off.

TO MAKE UP

Join the side and sleeve seams and stitch the sleeves into position. Join the ends of the neckband and stitch into position round the back of the neck.

Attach the buttons to correspond with buttonholes, using 3 strands of embroidery silk to sew 2 french knots in the middle of each, using the colours of your choice.

Following the Swiss darning instructions on page 114, work embroidery as indicated on the chart.

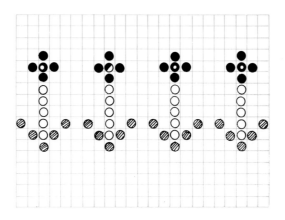

Swiss darning chart. One square represents one stitch.
Work each flower in a different colour.

NESTLING BLANKET
MATERIALS
1 metre (1 yard), white Viyella, Clydella or similar
4 metres (4 yards), pale green satin ribbon, 3 cm (1¼ in) wide, or pale green satin blanket binding
1 skein each of embroidery silks in green, yellow, pink, dark pink and pale blue

TO MAKE THE BLANKET

Open out the Viyella or Clydella into a single layer. Using tailor's chalk and a hard ruler, mark an 88 cm (35¼ in) square. Check the square is true by folding into a triangle. All raw edges should be of equal length. Cut out.

THE SATIN EDGING

1. Cut 2 pieces of ribbon, 88 cm (35¼ in) long.
2. Beginning at one corner, place 1.5 cm (⅝ in) of the ribbon, *wrong* side down, over the *right* side of the material edge. Pin down to the next corner and topstitch to the Viyella. Repeat with the other piece of ribbon on the opposite side edge.
3. Fold the excess 1.5 cm (⅝ in) of ribbon over to the *wrong* side of the material and pin in place. Slipstitch the ribbon to the machine-stitching line. Press with a cool iron.
4. Cut 2 pieces of ribbon 90 cm (36 in) long.
5. Fold under 1 cm (⅜ in) of ribbon at each end. Place 1.5 cm (⅝ in) of the ribbon *wrong* side down, over the *right* side of the material and covering the satin ribbon already in place at the corner. Pin down to the next corner and topstitch to the Viyella. Repeat with the remaining side and piece of ribbon. Turn the excess 1.5 cm (⅝ in) of ribbon over to the *wrong* side of the material and pin in place. (Thereby enclosing the raw edge of the satin already in place.) Slipstitch the ribbon to the machine-stitching line. Press with a cool iron.

THE EMBROIDERY

6. Enlarge the motifs to twice the size on to paper, using a black felt tip pen.
7. Working near a light or window, place the material over the enlarged pattern.
Using a pencil, trace the design on to the material. Embroider the design with 2 strands of embroidery silk, using the stitches and colours indicated.

Key to stitches:

stem stitch

lazy daisy stitch

satin stitch

large french knot

bullion knot

overstitch

TOP LEFT: *centre edge motif; middle left: corner motif; bottom left: middle of blanket motif; above: edge motifs*

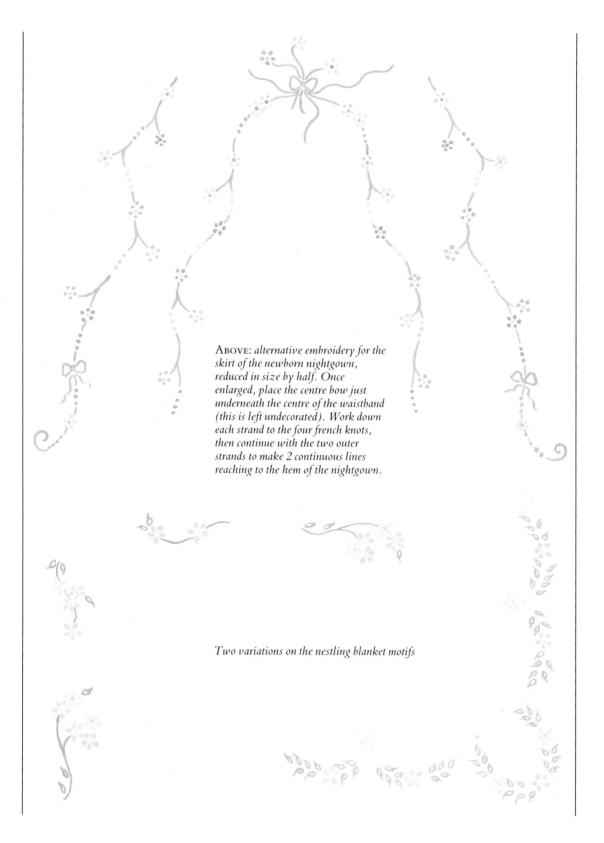

ABOVE: *alternative embroidery for the skirt of the newborn nightgown, reduced in size by half. Once enlarged, place the centre bow just underneath the centre of the waistband (this is left undecorated). Work down each strand to the four french knots, then continue with the two outer strands to make 2 continuous lines reaching to the hem of the nightgown.*

Two variations on the nestling blanket motifs

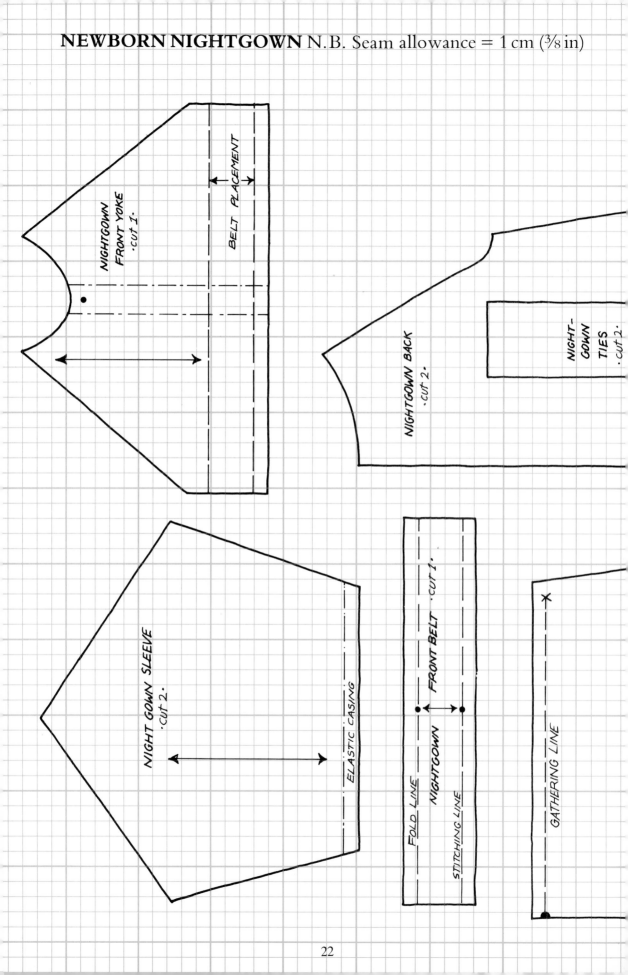

NEWBORN NIGHTGOWN N.B. Seam allowance = 1 cm (⅜ in)

NIGHTGOWN FRONT YOKE ·cut 1·

BELT PLACEMENT

NIGHTGOWN BACK ·cut 2·

NIGHT-GOWN TIES ·cut 2·

NIGHT GOWN SLEEVE ·cut 2·

ELASTIC CASING

FOLD LINE

FRONT BELT ·cut 1·

NIGHTGOWN

STITCHING LINE

GATHERING LINE

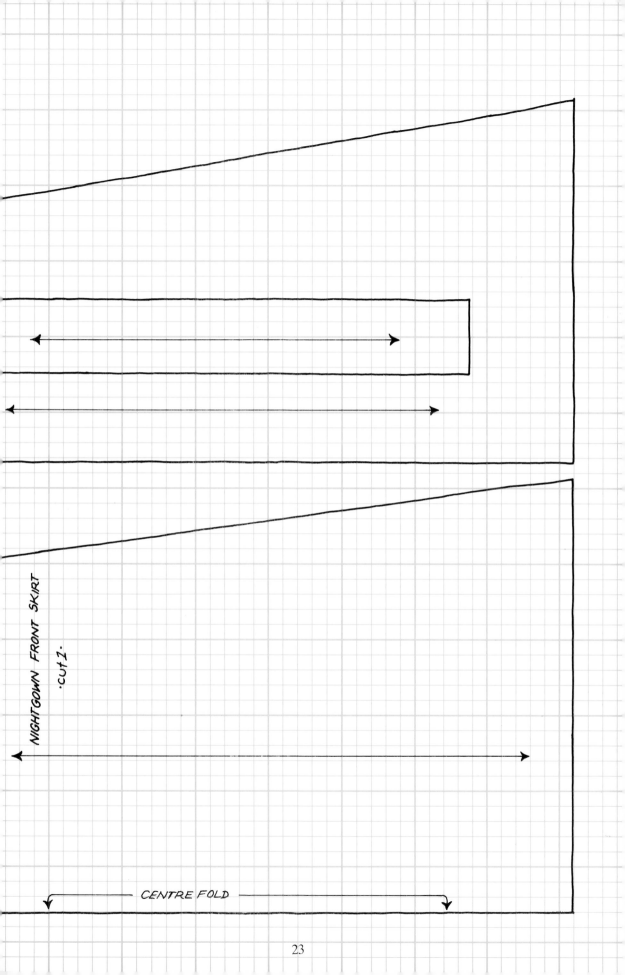

NIGHTGOWN FRONT SKIRT

·cut 1·

CENTRE FOLD

THREE MONTHS

Scolloped dress for a 3 month old (see page 26) made in cotton batiste for summer with a smocked nightgown (page 28) in Viyella for warmth.

THREE MONTHS

At three months, baby is just old enough for Nanny to put her into a dress during the daytime. Not so long ago, Nanny would even put a boy into a short dress like the one in the photograph on page 24 but this practice has now died out and a romper would be chosen. Bedtime, of course, means a nightgown for boy or girl.

With the advent of snowsuits and anoraks, pramcoats are sadly becoming a thing of the past. Nanny, however, likes to put her charge in a knitted pram set when she takes her out visiting or when taking her out for a walk in the pram. With the addition of a shawl or pram covers, baby is quite warm enough in this outfit and can be shown off easily, as she is not lost under bulky clothes. Nanny would put a boy in the same bonnet at this age and not a helmet-shaped cap. When he is a little older, he will wear a knitted round hat but never with a pompom on top.

The patterns for the pram set are made from a thicker wool – 4 ply – in order to give warmth. The pramcoat, bonnet and mittens are trimmed in a contrasting wool to match each other. The leggings have enough room to accommodate the nappy but the legs have been kept short, so that they do not trail beyond the baby's feet.

White is still the colour of choice for this age, with coloured embroidery used as before to relieve the plainness. It is amazing how easy scolloping is to do, even for the beginner, and how effective it is in making the garment look special. This dress pattern buttons all the way down the back to make it easy to put on: three month old babies tend to be very wriggly to dress! Room for growth has been allowed in the nightgown by the use of traditional smocking. As only one basic stitch is used in the smocking pattern, it is an easy project for someone who has not attempted this type of embroidery before.

SCOLLOPED DRESS

SIZE: 3 MONTHS

MATERIALS

1 metre (1 yard), cotton batiste, polyester cotton
or similar, 90 cm (36 in) wide or 70 cm (28 in)
× 115 cm (45 in) wide
50 cm (½ yard), white lace edging, 6 mm
(¼ in) wide
1 skein, pale blue embroidery silk
1 skein, pale yellow embroidery silk
scrap of pale green embroidery silk
8 small white buttons
1 small press-stud, size 00

THE PATTERN

Enlarge the pattern pieces given on pages 30 and 31. Following the diagrams on page 27, lay and cut out the pattern, including a 3 × 31 cm (1¼ × 12¼ in) bias strip for the binding around the neckline. Mark all dots, crosses and buttonholes with tailor's tacks.

THE SCOLLOPING AND THE EMBROIDERY

1. Mark the scollops on to the yoke front, back and cuffs. Embroider with 2 strands of yellow silk using the method described in the techniques section, page 116. Do not embroider the french knots yet.

2. Working near a light or window, place the skirt front over the enlarged Nestling Blanket motifs, page 20, and, using a pencil, trace the designs on to the material in the positions indicated leaving approximately 2.5 cm (1 in) between groups.

Repeat with the skirt backs. Embroider the design with 2 strands of embroidery silk, using the stitches indicated.

TO MAKE THE DRESS

JOINING THE YOKES AND SKIRTS

3. Make 2 rows of hand or machine gathering stitches between the dots on the top edge of the front and back skirts, as marked on the pattern.
4. Taking the skirt front, pull up the gathers until it is the same length as the yoke front. Repeat with the back yokes and skirts.
5. Place the *right* side of the front yoke *lining* and the *wrong* side of the front skirt together, matching centre dots. Pin the top edge of the skirt to the lower edge of the yoke lining, spreading the gathers evenly. Tack in place, then stitch across the seam and press towards the yoke. Remove the gathering threads. NB This leaves the raw edge of the seam on the *right* side of the garment.
6. Turn under 1 cm (⅜ in) along the selvage of the back skirts. Press in the back yoke linings along the fold line. Place the *right* side of the yoke linings and the *wrong* side of the skirt backs together. Pin the top edge of the skirts to the lower edge of the linings, spreading the gathers evenly. Tack in place, then stitch across the seam and press towards the yoke. Remove the gathering threads.
7. Join the yoke linings at the shoulders, *right* sides together, with a plain seam. Press open.
8. Join the side seams of the front and back skirts with a french seam. Press.
9. Join the front and back yokes at the shoulders, *right* sides together, with a plain seam. Press the seam open.
10. Aligning the corresponding shoulder seams, *wrong* sides together, pin, then tack the yoke lining to the yoke around the neckline.
11. Tack the yokes and linings together around the armholes. Slipstitch the lining to the yoke along the side edges of the backs.
12. Pin the scolloping over the seam lines on the front and backs. Using 3 strands of pale blue silk, sew in place with a french knot in the middle of each scollop.

THE SLEEVES

13. Make 2 rows of hand or machine gathering stitches between the crosses on the top and bottom edges of the sleeve, as marked on the pattern.
14. Pull up the gathers on the lower edge of the sleeve until it is the same length as the cuff. Spread the gathers evenly.
15. Join the sides of the sleeve with a french seam and the sides of the cuffs with a plain seam.
16. Pin the *right* side of the cuff to the *wrong* side of the sleeve, matching the centre dots, side seams and raw edges. Spread the gathers evenly and stitch the seam. Press cuff away from sleeve.
17. Fold the cuff over to the *right* side of the sleeve along the fold line. Press. Pin the scolloping over the seam line. Using 2 strands of pale blue embroidery silk, sew in place with a french knot in the middle of each scollop. The cuff should now be

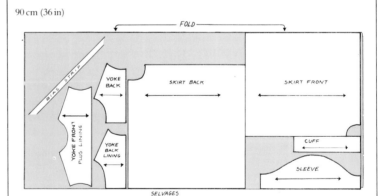

90 cm (36 in)

FOLD

BIAS STRIP

YOKE BACK

SKIRT BACK

SKIRT FRONT

YOKE FRONT PLUS LINING

YOKE BACK LINING

CUFF

SLEEVE

SELVAGES

115 cm (45 in)

FOLD

BIAS STRIP

CUFF

SKIRT FRONT

SKIRT BACK

YOKE FRONT + LINING

YOKE BACK LINING

YOKE BACK

SLEEVE

SELVAGES

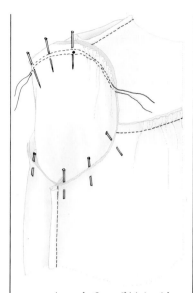

approximately 2 cm (¾ in) wide.
18. Turn the dress inside out and, with *right* sides together, align the side seams of the sleeve with the side seams of the skirt. Pin in

place, continue up the edges of the armhole until the gathering stitches are reached. Align the centre dot of the sleeve with the shoulder seam of the yoke and pin in place. Pull up the gathers until the sleeve fits the armhole and pin, see diagram. Tack around the armhole, then stitch.
19. Remove the gathering threads and press seam away from sleeve. Neaten the raw edges with machine whipping, or by hand with blanket stitch.

THE NECKLINE

20. With *right* sides together, pin the bias strip to the yoke neckline, turning in 1 cm (⅜ in) at each end. Stitch in place.
21. Trim the seam allowances, then fold the binding up over them to the inside of the yoke. Turn under the remaining edge of

the strip and pin to the seam line. Slipstitch in place.
22. Gather the lace and stitch it around the neckline where the binding joins the yoke.

THE HEM AND BACK

23. Turn in 1 cm (⅜ in) down the back skirt edges and press. Beginning at the neck, topstitch down the yoke near to the edge.
24. Turn under 2.5 cm (1 in) along the bottom edge of the skirt. Turn up another 3.5 cm (1⅜ in) to make a double hem and slipstitch in place.
25. Make buttonholes down the back in the positions shown on the pattern. Using 3 strands of embroidery silk, sew the buttons in position with 2 french knots, 1 yellow and 1 blue.
26. Sew a small press-stud on to neck bias.

A simpler embroidery motif for the dress made up of repeated daisies (see page 114).

SMOCKED NIGHTGOWN
Size: 3 months

MATERIALS
1.3 metres (1⅓ yards), white Viyella or similar, 90 cm (36 in) wide or 1 metre (1¼ yards) × 115 cm (45 in)
2.5 metres (2½ yards), white cotton lace edging, 6 mm (¼ in) wide
50 cm (½ yard), single cord elastic
1 skein, pale blue embroidery silk
2 small white buttons
1 small press-stud, size 00

THE PATTERN
Enlarge the pattern pieces given on pages 30 and 31. Following the diagrams on page 29, lay and cut out the pattern. Add the extra in the length of both skirts and in the centre front for smocking. Use the long sleeve pattern piece and cut a bias strip 3 × 31 cm (1¼ × 12¼ in) for the binding around the neckline. Mark all dots and buttonholes with tailor's tacks.

THE SMOCKING
1. Following the smocking instructions, page 116, make 7 rows of gathering on the front and back skirts. Pull up the gathering until the material is slightly

narrower than the corresponding yoke. Using 2 strands of silk, smock pattern A across the gathering, front and back.

TO MAKE THE NIGHTGOWN

2. Follow the instructions for the Smocked Dress, page 67, from step 3 to step 9 inclusive.

3. Make 2 rows of hand or machine gathering stitches between the crosses on the top edge of each sleeve, as marked on the pattern.

4. To finish the sleeves, follow steps 11 and 12 of the instructions for the Nightgown, page 15.

5. Continue with the instructions for the 12 month dress, from step 15 to step 21 inclusive.

6. Gather 50 cm (½ yard) of the lace and stitch it around the neckline where the binding joins the yoke.

7. Continue with steps 23 to 25 inclusive of the instructions for the 12 month dress, using pale blue embroidery silk to sew on the buttons.

8. Use the remaining lace to trim the hem of the nightgown.

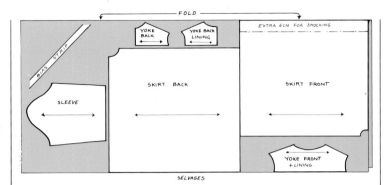

90 cm (36 in)

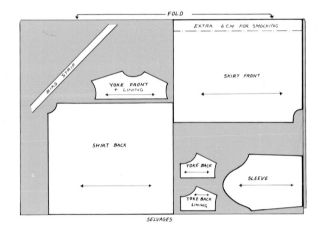

115 cm (45 in)

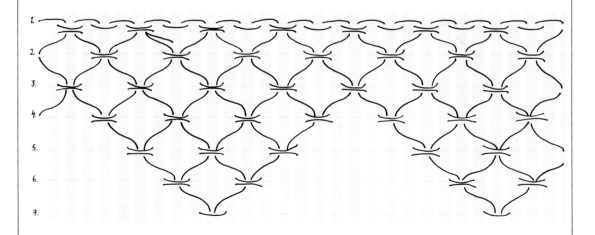

SMOCKING PATTERN A

3 MONTH DRESS & NIGHTGOWN N.B. Seam allowance = 1 cm (⅜ in)

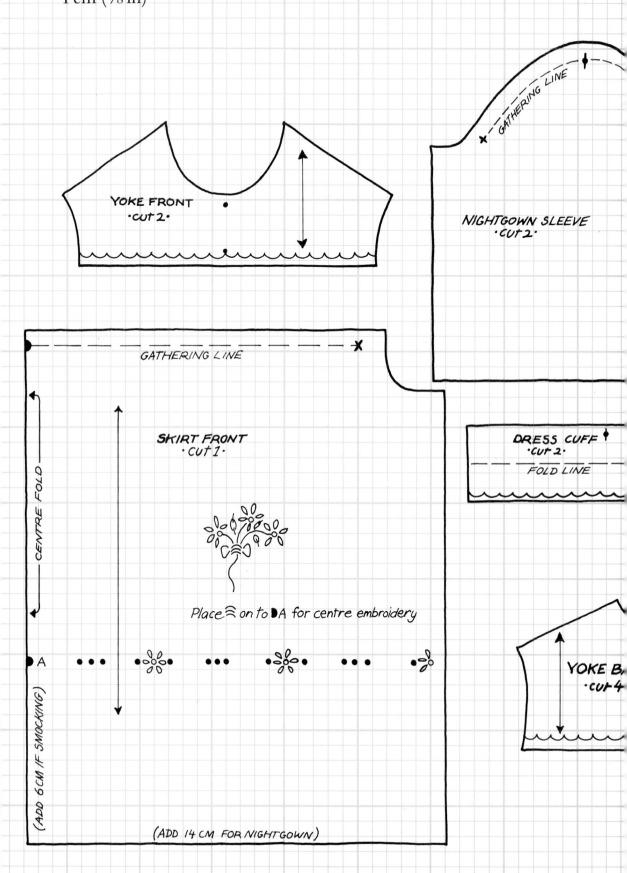

YOKE FRONT
·cut 2·

NIGHTGOWN SLEEVE
·cut 2·

GATHERING LINE

GATHERING LINE

SKIRT FRONT
·cut 1·

CENTRE FOLD

DRESS CUFF
·cut 2·

FOLD LINE

Place ≋ on to ▶A for centre embroidery

A

YOKE B
·cut 4

(ADD 6 CM IF SMOCKING)

(ADD 14 CM FOR NIGHTGOWN)

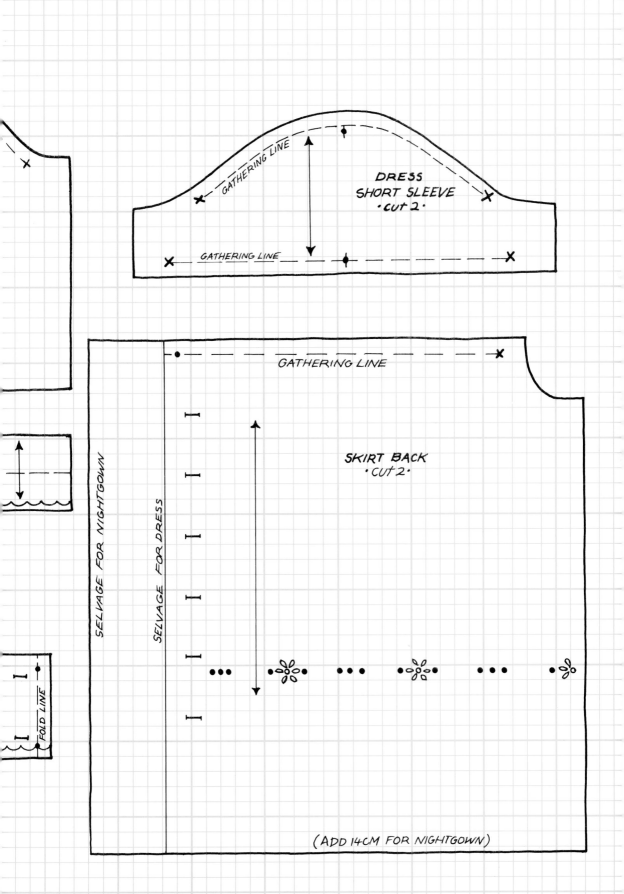

DRESS
SHORT SLEEVE
·cut 2·

GATHERING LINE

GATHERING LINE

GATHERING LINE

SKIRT BACK
·cut 2·

SELVAGE FOR NIGHTGOWN

SELVAGE FOR DRESS

FOLD LINE

(ADD 14CM FOR NIGHTGOWN)

*Pram set for a 3 month old baby: pram coat (see page 34) and leggings (page 36)
with matching bonnet and mittens (page 37). All are knitted in 4 ply.*

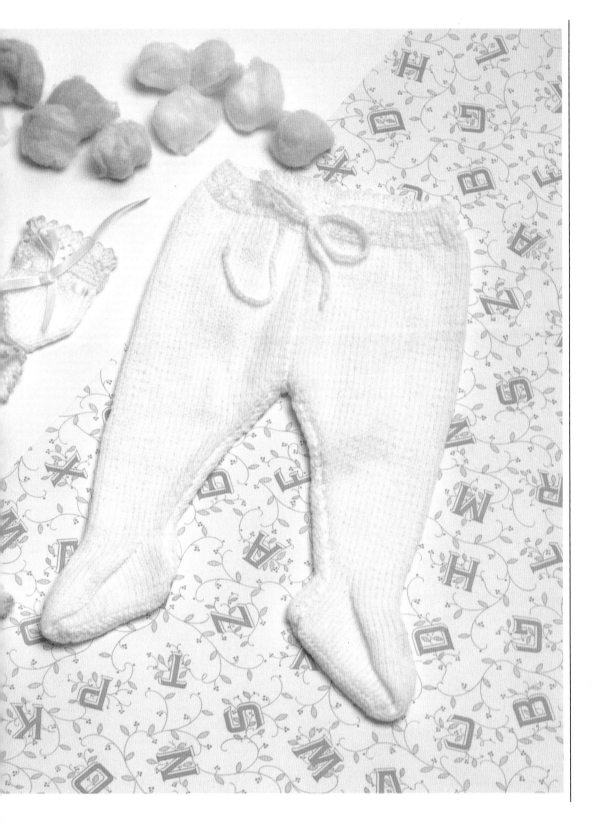

PRAM COAT

SIZE: 3 MONTHS

MATERIALS

120 grams (5 oz) × 4 ply, white wool
scrap of 4 ply, pale blue wool
scrap of pale blue embroidery silk
6 small white buttons with star-shaped cut-out
1 pair each 3¼ mm & 3¾ mm (nos. 10 & 9)
needles

RIGHT FRONT

Using 3¼ mm (no. 10) needles and the two needle method, cast on 63 sts.
Row 1: knit.
Row 2: purl.
Row 3: change to blue wool, k1, ★ yfwd, k2tog, repeat from ★ to end of row.
Row 4: change back to white wool and purl 1 row.
Rows 5 and 6: as rows 1 and 2.
Row 7: make scolloping: fold work in half to *wrong* side, knit first stitch on needle together with corresponding loop from cast-on edge as shown in the diagram (see right).
Continue knitting together one stitch from needle with corresponding loop all across the row.
Row 8: knit (thus making a ridge).
Change to 3¾ mm (no. 9) needles and carry on in lace pattern with moss st border:
Row 9: k1, p1, k1, p1, k3, ★ yfwd, sl.1, k2tog, psso, yfwd, k1, repeat from ★ to end of row.
Row 10 and alt. rows: k1, purl to last 5 sts, k1, p1, k1, p1, k1.
Row 11: k1, p1, k1, p1, k2, ★ k5, yfwd, sl.1, k2tog, psso, yfwd, repeat from ★ to last st, k1.
Row 13: as row 11.
Row 15: k1, p1, k1, p1, k2, ★ yfwd, sl.1, k1, psso, k1, k2tog, yfwd, k3, repeat from ★ to last st, k1.
Row 16: as row 10.
Rows 9 to 16 form the pattern.

Repeat rows 9 to 16 inclusive, 8 times more.
Next row: k1, p1, k1, p1, k1, ★ (k2tog, 4 times), k1, repeat from ★ to last 4 sts, (k2tog, twice). (37 sts.)
Moss st 3 rows.
Next row: k1, k2tog, yrn, moss st 12, k2tog, yrn, moss st to end of row.
Moss st 3 rows.
Next row: k1, p1, k1, p1, knit to end of row.
Next row: k1, purl to last 5 sts, k1, p1, k1, p1, k1.
Next row: k1, p1, k1, p1, knit to end of row.
Keeping moss stitch border correct, shape armhole by casting off 3 sts at beginning of next row. Decrease 1 st at armhole edge on next 3 rows. (31 sts.)
Work 10 rows in stocking st with moss st border, working buttonholes as before on 2nd row.
Next row: k1, purl to last 19 sts, moss st 19.
Next row: moss st 19, knit to end of row.
Next row: k1, purl to last 19 sts, moss st 19.
Next row: k1, k2tog, yrn, moss st 12, k2tog, yrn, p1, knit to end of row.
Next row: k1, purl to last 19 sts, moss st 19.
Next row: moss st 19 sts, knit to end.
Next row: k1, purl to last 19 sts, moss st 19.

SHAPING NECK

Cast off 14 sts, moss st 5, knit to end.
Next row: k1, p1, to last 5 sts, moss st 5.
★★ Keeping moss st border at neck edge correct, continue on these sts for 7 rows, finishing at armhole edge.
Next row: cast off 6 sts, work to end.
Next row: work to end.
Next row: cast off 6 sts, work to end. (5 sts.)
Moss st 15 rows.
Cast off.

LEFT FRONT

Using 3¼ mm (no. 10) needles and the two needle method, cast on 63 sts.
Row 1: knit.
Row 2: purl.
Row 3: change to blue wool, k1, ★ yfwd, k2tog, repeat from ★ to end of row.
Row 4: change back to white wool and purl.
Rows 5 and 6: as rows 1 and 2.
Row 7: make scolloping: fold work in half to *wrong* side, knit first stitch on needle together with corresponding loop from cast-on edge. Continue knitting together one stitch from needle with corresponding loop all across the row.
Row 8: knit.
Change to 3¾ mm (no. 9) needles and carry on in lace pattern with moss st border as follows:

Row 9: k2, ★ yfwd, sl.1, k2tog, psso, yfwd, k1, repeat from ★ to last 5 sts, k1, p1, k1, p1, k1.
Row 10: k1, p1, k1, p1, k1, purl to last st, k1.
Row 11: k2, ★ yfwd, sl.1, k2tog, psso, yfwd, k5, repeat from ★ to last 5 sts, k1, p1, k1, p1, k1.
Row 12: as row 10.
Row 13: as row 11.
Row 14: as row 10.
Row 15: k5, ★ yfwd, sl.1, k1, psso, k1, k2tog, yfwd, k3, repeat from ★ to last 10 sts, yfwd, sl.1, k1, psso, k1, k2tog, yfwd, k1, p1, k1, p1, k1.
Row 16: as row 10.
Repeat rows 9 to 16 inclusive, 8 times more.
Next row: (k2tog twice), ★ k1, (k2tog, 4 times), repeat from ★ to last 5 sts, moss st 5.
Moss st 7 rows.
Next row: knit to last 5 sts, moss st 5.
Next row: moss st 5, purl to last st, k1.
Keeping moss st border correct as on last 2 rows, shape armhole by casting off 3 sts at beginning of next row.
Dec. 1 st at armhole edge on next 3 rows. (31 sts.)
Keeping moss st border correct, work 11 rows in stocking st.
Next row: moss st 19, purl to last st, k1.
Next row: knit to last 19 sts, moss st 19.
Repeat last 2 rows twice.
Next row: cast off 14 sts (1 st on needle after cast-off), moss st 4, purl to last st, k1.
Next row: knit to last 5 sts, moss st 5.
Complete to match right front, working ★★ to end.

BACK

Using 3¼ mm (no. 10) needles and the two needle method, cast on 95 sts.
Work rows 1 to 8 as on right front.

Change to 3¾ mm (no. 9) needles.
Row 9: k2, ★ yfwd, sl.1, k2tog, psso, yfwd, k1, repeat from ★ to last st, k1.
Row 10: k1, purl to last st, k1.
Row 11: k1, ★ k5, yfwd, sl.1, k2tog, psso, yfwd, repeat from ★ to last 6 sts, k6.
Row 12: as row 10.
Row 13: as row 11.
Row 14: as row 10.
Row 15: k1, ★ yfwd, sl.1, k1, psso, k1, k2tog, yfwd, k3, repeat from ★ to last 6 sts, yfwd, sl.1, k1, psso, k1, k2tog, yfwd, k1.
Row 16: as row 10.
Rows 9 to 16 form the pattern.
Repeat rows 9 to 16 inclusive, 8 times more.
Next row: k1, p1, k1, ★ (k2tog, 4 times), k1, repeat from ★ to last 2 sts, k2. (55 sts.)
Moss st 7 rows.
Next row: knit.
Next row: k1, purl to last st, k1.
Shape armholes by casting off 3 sts at beginning of next 2 rows.
Dec. 1 st at both ends of following 3 rows.
Continue in stocking st for 25 rows.
Shape shoulders by casting off 6 sts at beginning of next 4 rows.
Cast off.

SLEEVES

Using 3¼ mm (no. 10) needles and two needle method, cast on 27 sts.
Work rows 1 to 8 as for right front.
Change to 3¾ mm (no. 9) needles and moss st 7 rows.
Next row: p3 (inc. in next st, p3), repeat brackets to end. (33 sts.)
Proceed in stocking st, increasing 1 st in 2nd st, and last but one st, on 5th and every following 6th row, until there are 41 sts.
Continue without increasing for 11 more rows.
Shape top by casting off 2 sts at beginning of next 2 rows.
Dec. 1 st at both ends of next and every alt. row until 29 sts remain, then dec. 1 st at both ends of every row until 9 sts remain.
Cast off.

TO MAKE UP

Join the shoulder seams, then side and sleeve seams.
Stitch the sleeves into position.
Sew the ends of the bands together. Stitch into position across the back of the neck.
Sew the buttons in corresponding places to buttonholes with 2 french knots and using 3 strands of pale blue embroidery silk.

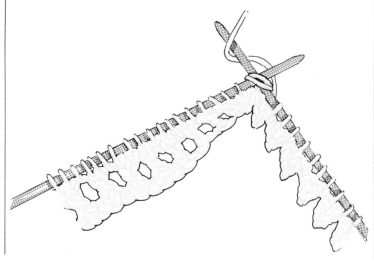

LEGGINGS

Size: 3 months
MATERIALS
60 grams (3 oz) × 4 ply, white wool
1 pair each 3¼ mm & 3¾ mm (nos. 10 & 9)
needles

RIGHT LEG

Using 3¼ mm (no. 10) needles, cast on 55 sts.
Rib 4 rows.
Next row: k1, * yfwd, k2tog, k1, repeat from * to end of row.
Rib 3 rows.
Change to 3¾ mm (no. 9) needles. Work 2 rows in st. st, beginning with a knit row.

SHAPING BACK

Row 1: knit 10 sts, turn,
Row 2 and alt. rows: sl.1, purl to end of row.
Row 3: knit 16 sts, turn,
Continue to work 6 sts more on every alt. knit row until the row knit 34, turn, has been worked.
Next row: sl.1, purl to end of row.
Continue in stocking st and work 4 rows across all sts. Inc. 1 st at the beginning (back edge) of next and every following 6th row, 6 times in all. (61 sts.)
Work 7 rows ending with a purl row.

SHAPING LEG

Dec. 1 st at each end of next 3 rows. (55 sts.)
Work 1 row straight.
Dec. 1 st at each end of next and every alt. row, 6 times in all (43 sts), then every following 4th row until 29 sts.
Purl 1 row.

SHAPING INSTEP

Row 1: knit 25 sts, turn,
Row 2: purl 14 sts, turn,
Work 16 rows in stocking stitch on these 14 stitches.
Break yarn and rejoin to inside edge, after the 11 sts. With *right*

side facing pick up and knit 14 sts along side edge, k14, pick up and knit 14 sts along remaining side edge and knit across remaining sts. (57 sts.)
Stocking st 9 rows.

SHAPING SOLE

Row 1: k3, k2tog, k1, k2tog, k21, k2tog, k2, k2tog, knit to end of row.
Row 2: purl.
Row 3: k2, k2tog, k1, k2tog, k19, k2tog, k2, k2tog, knit to end of row.
Row 4: purl.
Row 5: k1, k2tog, k1, k2tog, k17, k2tog, k2, k2tog, knit to end.
Row 6: purl.
Cast off.

LEFT LEG

Using 3¼ mm (no. 10) needles, cast on 55 sts.
Rib 4 rows.
Next row: k1, * yfwd, k2tog, k1, repeat from * to end of row.
Rib 3 rows.
Change to 3¾ mm (no. 9) needles and knit one row.

SHAPING BACK

Row 1: purl 10 sts, turn,
Row 2 and alt. rows: sl.1, knit to end of row.
Row 3: purl 16 sts, turn,
Continue to work 6 sts more on every alt. row until the row purl 34 sts, turn, has been worked.
Next row: sl.1, knit to end.
Continuing in stocking st, work 4 rows across all sts. Inc. 1 st at beginning (back edge) of next and every following 6th row, 6 times in all. (61 sts.)

Work 8 rows in stocking st ending with a purl row.

SHAPING LEG

Dec. 1 st at each end of next 3 rows. (55 sts.)
Work one row straight.
Dec. 1 st at each end of next and every alt. row 6 times in all (43 sts), then every following 4th row until 29 sts.
Work one row straight.

SHAPING INSTEP

Knit 18 sts, turn,
Purl 14 sts, turn,
Work 16 rows in stocking st on these 14 sts.
Break yarn and rejoin to inside edge. With *right* side facing, pick up and knit 14 sts along the side edge, k14, pick up and knit 14 sts along remaining side edge and knit across remaining sts.
Stocking st 9 rows.

SHAPING SOLE

Row 1: k22, k2tog, k2, k2tog, k21, k2tog, k1, k2tog, k3.
Row 2: purl.
Row 3: k21, k2tog, k2, k2tog, k19, k2tog, k1, k2tog, k2.
Row 4: purl.
Row 5: k20, k2tog, k2, k2tog, k17, k2tog, k1, k2tog, k1.
Row 6: purl.
Cast off.

TO MAKE UP

Join the front, back, leg and foot seams. Make a cord by chain stitching with a crochet hook. Thread the cord through the eyelets in the ribbing.

BONNET

Size: 3 months
MATERIALS
20 grams (1 oz) × 4 ply, white wool
10 grams (½ oz) × 4 ply, pale blue wool
1 metre (1 yard) white satin ribbon, 1.5 cm
(⅝ in) wide
1 pair 3¾ mm (no. 9) needles

Cast on 73 sts.
Knit 2 rows.
Row 1: k2, * yfwd, k2tog, repeat from * to last st, k1.
Row 2 and alt. rows: knit.
Row 3: k2, * k1, (yfwd, k2tog,) work brackets 6 times, k1, repeat from * to last st, k1.
Row 5: k2, * k2, (yfwd, k2tog,) work brackets 5 times, k2, repeat from * to last st, k1.
Row 7: k2, * k3, (yfwd, k2tog,) work brackets 4 times, k3, repeat from * to last st, k1.
Row 9: k2, * k4, (yfwd, k2tog,) work brackets 3 times, k4, repeat from * to last st, k1.
Row 11: k2, * k5, (yfwd, k2tog,) work brackets twice, k5, repeat from * to last st, k1.

Row 13: k2, * k6, yfwd, k2tog, k6, repeat from * to last st, k1.
Row 14: knit.
Row 15: knit.
Row 16: purl.
Rib 6 rows, changing from white to blue wool on 2nd row.
Stocking st 4 rows.
Next row: k1, k2tog, k33, k2tog, k32, k2tog, k1. (70 sts.)
Purl 1 row.
Change back to white wool and stocking st 20 rows.
Next row: * k2tog, k8, repeat from * to end of row.
Next row and alt. rows: knit.
Next row: * k2tog, k7, repeat from * to end of row.
Next row: * k2tog, k6, repeat from * to end of row.

Continue decreasing in this manner until k2tog, k1, and the following knit row is done.
Next row: k2tog, repeat to the last st, k1.
Draw thread through remaining stitches and fasten off securely.

TO MAKE UP
Sew the two sides together down to just below the crown shaping (approximately 8 cm (3¼ in) in all).
Turn the front pattern over the blue band and sew in place at the side edges (approximately 4.5 cm (1¾ in)).
Cut the satin ribbon in half and sew a piece to each side of the bonnet.

MITTENS

Size and materials as for Bonnet, except only scrap of pale blue wool needed

Cast on 32 sts, using the two needle method.
Row 1: knit.
Row 2: purl.
Row 3: change to blue wool, k1, * yfwd, k2tog, repeat from * to last st, k1.
Row 4: change back to white wool and purl 1 row.
Row 5: knit.
Row 6: purl.
Row 7: make scolloping (see diagram, page 35): fold work in half to *wrong* side, knit first stitch on needle together with corresponding loop from cast-on edge. Continue knitting together one stitch from needle with corresponding loop to end.
Row 8: k1, * k1, (yfwd, k2tog),

work brackets 4 times, k1, repeat from * to last st, k1.
Row 9 and alt. rows: knit.
Row 10: k1, * k2, (yfwd, k2tog), work brackets 3 times, k2, repeat from * to last st, k1.
Row 12: k1, * k3, (yfwd, k2tog), work brackets twice, k3, repeat from * to last st, k1.
Row 14: k1, *k4, yfwd, k2tog, k4, repeat from * to last st, k1.
Rows 15 and 16: knit.
Row 17: purl.
Row 18: k1, (k1, yfwd, k2tog), work brackets 10 times, k1.
Row 19: purl.
Stocking stitch 12 more rows.

SHAPING TOP
Row 1: * k1, k2tog tb1, k10,

k2tog, k1, repeat from * to end of row.
Row 2 and alt. rows: k1, purl to last st, k1.
Row 3: * k1, k2tog tb1, k8, k2tog, k1, repeat from * to end of row.
Row 5: * k1, k2tog tb1, k6, k2tog, k1, repeat from * to end of row.
Row 7: * k1, k2tog tb1, k4, k2tog, k1, repeat from * to end of row.
Row 8: as row 2.
Cast off.

TO MAKE UP
Join the side seam. Cut the ribbon in half and thread through the eyelets in the wrist of each mitten.

SIX MONTHS

traditional Nanny would tend not to put her charge into the stretch suits and the disposable nappies that are available as all-in-one day clothes. She would choose a smocked romper suit or dress, cardigan and bootees. Towelling nappies would be used, except perhaps for convenience when travelling, and this style of dress helps to avoid the 'skinned rabbit' look that babies of this age can have.

Nanny always smocks a romper suit or a dress at the back as well as the front, since babies are so often seen from behind when carried. For this reason, too, dresses are always made long enough to cover the nappy, which would not be allowed to show. Pale coloured materials may now be introduced into the wardrobe for everyday wear, although Nanny still prefers white for smart occasions. She chooses bootees to keep baby's feet warm in the winter, embroidered to match the cardigan. Socks definitely do not appear until the baby is much older. This rule stems from the 1920s when many more people had nannies to look after their children and socks were snobbishly thought to be a sign that a family did not have a nanny to knit for their baby. Few people even know the reason why now but the old rule still remains.

The romper suit is once again made from Viyella for warmth and, as a boy would not want his romper trimmed with lace, there is embroidery round the neck and cuffs picked out in a colour to relieve the plainness. The dress is in a lightweight material for the summer, elegantly trimmed with a dainty lace edging and smocked at front and back. The buttons are sewn on with french knots in two colours. This has the double advantage of being a feature when the baby is seen from the back, as well as matching the buttons on the cardigan. The cardigan and bootees in this section are embroidered with the same coloured silks as the romper suit and dress, so that the whole outfit for boy and girl harmonizes.

SMOCKED ROMPER
Size: 6 months
MATERIALS

1.1 metres (1¼ yards), pale blue Viyella, Clydella or similar, 90 cm (36 in) or 1 metre (1⅙ yards) × 115 cm (45 in)
50 cm (½ yard), narrow elastic, 6 mm (¼ in) wide
1 skein, pale blue embroidery silk
1 skein, blue embroidery silk
1 skein, white embroidery silk
7 small white buttons with star-shaped cut-out and 2 plain white buttons
1 small press-stud, size 00

THE PATTERN
Enlarge the pattern pieces given on pages 45, 46 and 47. Following the diagrams on page 39, lay and cut out the pattern, including a 3 × 31 cm (1¼ × 12¼ in) bias strip for the binding around the neckline.

Mark all dots, crosses and buttonholes with tailor's tacks. For pintucked yoke cut 1 D yoke front and 1 C yoke front. For plain yoke cut 2 D yoke fronts.

THE SMOCKING
1. Make and stitch pintucks in front yoke following the instructions in the techniques section, page 108, if working this version.
2. Following the smocking instructions, page 116, make 15

rows of gathering on the front skirt and 11 rows on the skirt backs, being careful to place the smocking dots to avoid the buttons and buttonholes. Pull up the gathering until the material is slightly narrower than the corresponding yoke. (If the yoke front is to have pintucks these should be stitched in place before gathering the skirt.) Using 2 strands of embroidery silk, smock and embroider pattern B across the gathering. Smock and embroider the shortened version on the backs (rows 3 to 13).

TO MAKE THE ROMPER

JOINING THE YOKES AND SKIRTS

3. Place the *right* sides of the front yoke and the front skirt together, matching centre dots. Pin the top edge of the smocking to the lower edge of the yoke, spreading the fullness evenly. Tack in place, then stitch across the seam. Press the seam towards the yoke.

SMOCKING PATTERN B: *rows 1, 3, 4, 12, 13, 15 in pale blue, rest in white with blue french knots, pale blue bullion knots and blue lazy daisy stitches. Work rows 3 to 13 only on backs.*

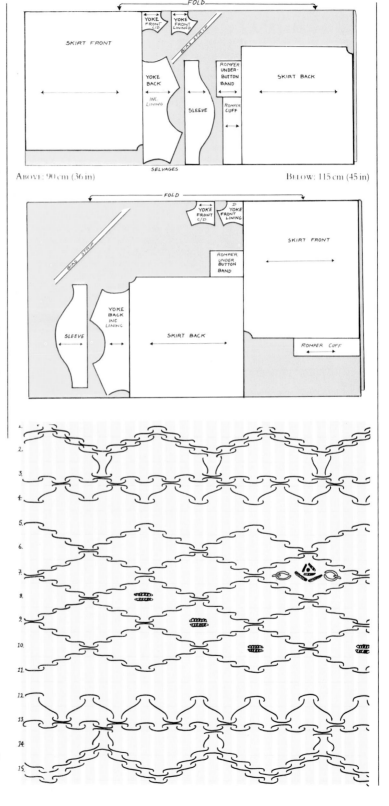

ABOVE: 90 cm (36 in)   BELOW: 115 cm (45 in)

SIX MONTHS

Winter romper suit (see page 38) for a 6 month old boy and summer dress (page 44) made from the same pattern for a girl of the same age.

4. With *right* sides together, align the left back yoke with the left back skirt. Pin the top edge of the smocking to the lower edge of the yoke, again spreading the fullness evenly. Make sure that the centre dots are matching and allow the yoke lining to extend beyond the skirt edge, see diagram (i). Tack the lining in place and stitch across the seam. Press the seam towards the yoke.

5. Repeat the procedure with the right back yoke and skirt.

6. Remove all the guide threads from the smocking.

7. Join the front and back yokes at the shoulders, *right* sides together, with a plain seam, leaving the lining of the back yokes hanging free, see diagram (ii). Press the seam open.

8. Using a french seam join the side seams of the front and back skirts. Press.

THE SLEEVES

9. Make 2 rows of hand or machine gathering stitches between the crosses on the top and bottom edges of the sleeve, as marked on the pattern.

10. Pull up the gathers on the lower edge of the sleeve until it is the same length as the cuff. Spread the gathers evenly.

11. Pin the cuff and sleeve together along this edge, *right* sides together, matching centre dots. Stitch in place. Trim the seam allowance and press downwards.

12. Join the side edges of the cuff/sleeve with a french seam.

13. Fold the cuff in half along the line as marked on the pattern. On the inside turn under the remaining seam allowance and pin to the seam line. Slipstitch in place. The cuff should now be 2 cm (¾ in) wide. Press.

14. Turn the romper inside out and, with *right* sides together, align the side seams of the sleeve

(i)

with the side seams of the skirt. Pin in place, continue up the edges of the armhole until the gathering stitches are reached. Align the centre dot of the sleeve with the shoulder seam of the yoke and pin in place. Pull up the gathers until the sleeve fits the armhole and pin. Tack around the armhole, then stitch the seam.

15. Remove the gathering threads and press away from sleeve. Neaten the lower edges of the armhole seam, between the front and back yokes, with machine whipping, or by hand with blanket stitch.

THE LINING

16. Join the back yoke lining to the front yoke lining at the shoulders, *right* sides together, with a plain seam. Press the seam open.

17. Fold the lining over and, with *wrong* sides together, pin, then tack the yoke lining to the yoke around the neckline, aligning the corresponding shoulder seams.

18. On the inside, turn under the seam allowances on the front and back yoke lining. Press the yoke/sleeve inwards and pin the lining over this and the yoke/skirt seams. Slipstitch in place (thus enclosing all raw edges).

THE BACK

19. Neaten the back skirt edges if they have not been cut on the selvage.

(ii)

20. Turn in 1 cm (⅜ in) along skirt edge and pin. Beginning at the neck, topstitch down yoke and skirt as near to the edge as possible.

21. Place left side over the right, aligning B on top of A. Pin and stitch on top of previous top stitching from B down to the hem.

THE NECKLINE

22. With *right* sides together, pin the bias strip to the yoke neckline, turning in 1 cm (⅜ in) at each end. Stitch in place.

23. Trim the seam allowances, then fold the binding up over them to the inside of the yoke. Turn under the remaining edge of the strip and pin to the seam line. Slipstitch in place.

THE LEG CASING AND BUTTONBANDS

24. Make a narrow 1 cm (⅜ in) casing along the bottom edge, leaving 7.5 cm (3 in) free at the centre front and back, as marked on the pattern.

25. Thread 18 cm (7 in) elastic (adjust here if necessary to width of the baby's leg plus 2 cm / ¾ in) through the leg casings and secure with several stitches.
26. Returning to the centre, press the seam allowance between the leg casings up, turning under the raw edge.
27. With *right* sides together, align the bottom edge of the front under-buttonband with the fold between the leg casings. Match centre dots and turn in the side

edges. Pin, then tack in place. Stitch across the band at the same level as the bottom row of stitching for the leg casings, see diagram (iii).
28. Fold the band in half along the line, as marked on the pattern, over the seam allowance to the inside. Turn under the remaining edge of the band and pin to the seam line. Slipstitch in place. The band should now be 9 cm (3½ in) wide and should cover the stitches holding the elastic in place, see

diagram (iv).
29. Repeat the procedure for the back under-buttonband.
30. On the front under-buttonband, make 2 buttonholes where indicated.
31. Using ordinary sewing thread, sew the 2 plain buttons on the back under-buttonband in corresponding places to the buttonholes.

FINISHING THE ROMPER

32. Make buttonholes down the back in the positions shown on the pattern. Using 3 strands of blue embroidery silk, sew buttons in position with 2 french knots.
33. Using 2 strands of white embroidery silk, feather stitch around the neckline and the cuffs.
34. Sew a small press-stud on the neck bias.

(iii)

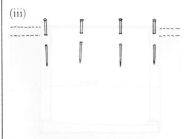

(iv)

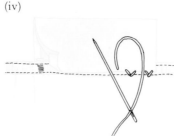

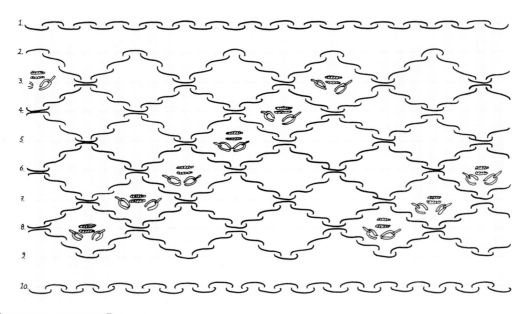

SMOCKING PATTERN C: *in pale pink with pink bullion knots and pale green lazy daisy stitches. Work rows 1 to 6, then row 10 on backs.*

SMOCKED DRESS

SIZE: 6 MONTHS

MATERIALS

*1.3 metres (1½ yards), Swiss cotton satin stripe
voile, cotton lawn, polyester cotton or similar,
90 cm (36 in) wide or 1.2 metres (1⅓ yards) ×
115 cm (45 in)
1.25 metres (1⅓ yards) white lace edging,
13 mm (½ in) wide
1 skein, pale pink embroidery silk
1 skein, pink embroidery silk
1 skein, pale green embroidery silk
2 small white buttons, with star-shaped cut-out
1 small press-stud, size 00*

THE PATTERN

Enlarge the pattern pieces given on pages 45, 46 and 47. Lay and cut out the pattern as for the romper, omitting the cuff and under-buttonband and making certain that the correct length of skirt is chosen. Use yoke front D and cut out 3 bias strips one 3 × 36 cm (1¼ in × 14¼ in) for the binding around the neckline and two 3 × 20 cm (1¼ × 8 in) for the sleeve edging. Mark all dots, crosses and buttonholes with tailor's tacks.

THE SMOCKING

1. Following the smocking instructions, page 116, make 10 rows of gathering on the front skirt and 7 rows on the skirt backs. Pull up the gathering until the material is slightly narrower than the corresponding yoke. Using 2 strands of embroidery silk, smock pattern C across the gathering. Smock the shortened version on the backs (rows 1 to 6, then row 10). Work embroidery in between smocking rows as shown.

TO MAKE THE DRESS

2. Follow the instructions for the Smocked Dress for a 12 month old, page 66, from step 3 to step 10 inclusive.
3. Pull up the gathers on the lower edge of the sleeve until it is the same length as one of the bias strips for the sleeve – 3 × 20 cm (1¼ × 8 in). Spread the gathers evenly.
4. Join the side edges of the sleeve with a french seam.
5. Finish the sleeve with bias binding and repeat for the second seam.
6. Continue with the instructions for the 12 month dress, from step 15 to step 21 inclusive.
7. Gather 55 cm (20 in) of lace and stitch it around the neckline where the binding joins the yoke.
8. Continue with step 23 of the instructions for the 12 month dress.
9. Gather 35 cm (14 in) of lace and stitch it around the armhole where the binding joins the sleeve. Embroider 3 rosebuds in the centre of the bias. Repeat with the 2nd armhole.
10. Embroider 3 rosebuds, centre front, on the neck binding.
11. Make buttonholes down the back in the positions shown on the pattern. Sew the 2 buttons in place with 2 french knots, 1 pink and 1 green, using 3 strands of embroidery silk. This makes a small fold in the skirt when the buttons are fastened.
12. Sew a small press-stud on the neck bias.

An alternative embroidered design for the skirt of the romper suit. Follow the stitch key on page 20.

6 MONTH ROMPER SUIT & DRESS N.B. Seam allowance = 1 cm (⅜ in)

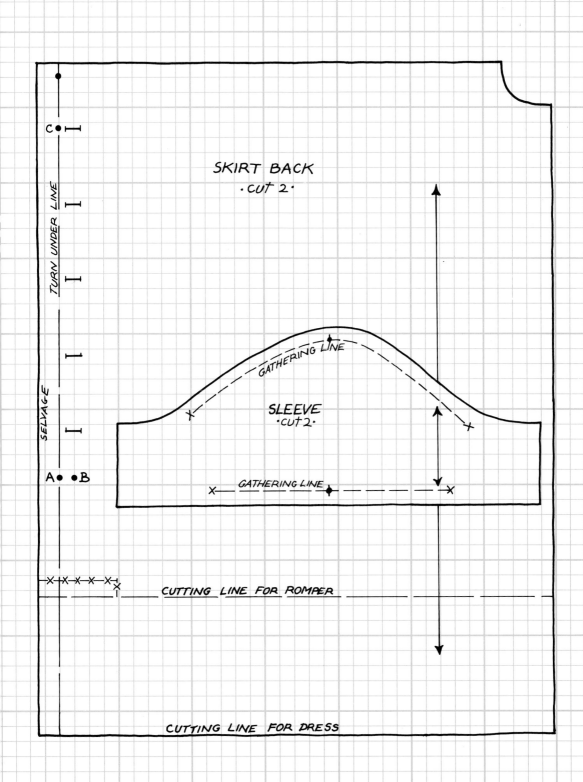

SKIRT BACK
·CUT 2·

C

TURN UNDER LINE

SELVAGE

A● ●B

GATHERING LINE

SLEEVE
·CUT 2·

GATHERING LINE

CUTTING LINE FOR ROMPER

CUTTING LINE FOR DRESS

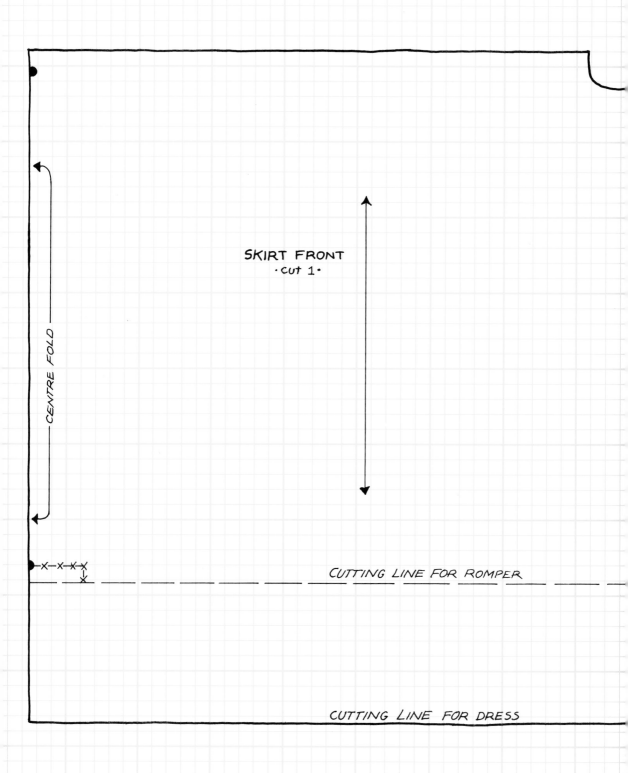

SKIRT FRONT
·cut 1·

CENTRE FOLD

CUTTING LINE FOR ROMPER

CUTTING LINE FOR DRESS

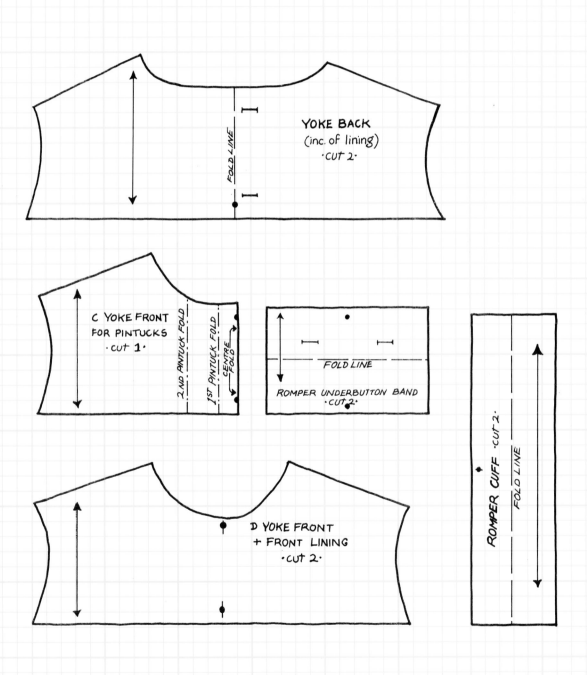

YOKE BACK
(inc. of lining)
·CUT 2·

FOLD LINE

C YOKE FRONT
FOR PINTUCKS
·CUT 1·

2ND PINTUCK FOLD

1ST PINTUCK FOLD

CENTRE FOLD

FOLD LINE

ROMPER UNDERBUTTON BAND
·CUT 2·

D YOKE FRONT
+ FRONT LINING
·CUT 2·

ROMPER CUFF ·CUT 2·

FOLD LINE

*Embroidered cardigan (see page 54) and bootees (page 55) to match the dress for
a 6 month old. The bibs (page 50) are for special occasions.*

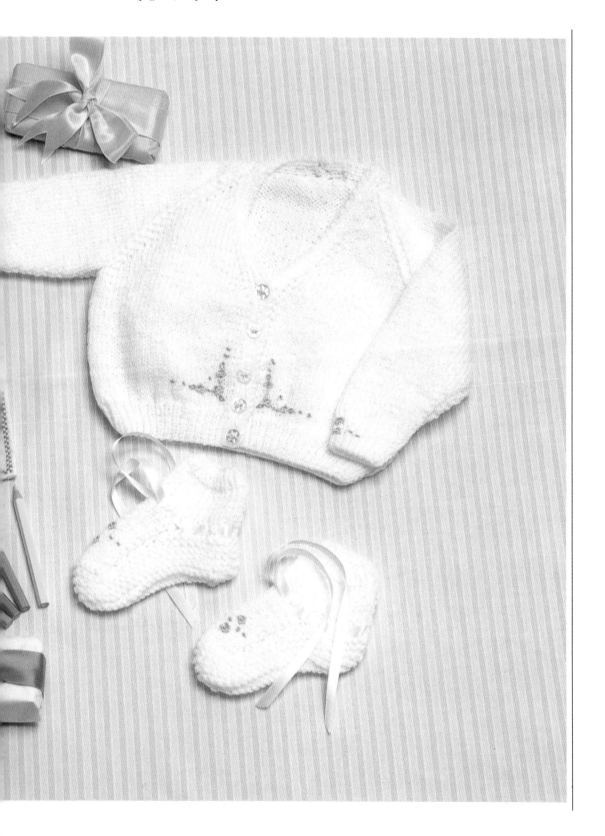

MATCHING OUTFITS

As well as making a whole outfit that tones, Nanny ensures that as far as possible, all her charges are dressed alike. This is quite easy when all the children are of the same sex, as the same garments can be made in the relevant sizes.

For two boys aged 18 months and three years Nanny may, for example, make a buster suit with red button-on pants for the younger boy and a version with red short trousers (as shown in the photograph on page 88) for the elder.

For three little girls, the apricot dress and cardigan (page 80) could be made in the required sizes. If three dresses were to be made to the same pattern, Nanny may occasionally work a different smocking pattern in the same colours on each dress. Another possibility would be to work the same smocking pattern on the same material but to use a different shade of embroidery silk for each one, thus giving individuality and variety to each dress.

It is less straightforward to dress brothers and sisters alike. This problem is solved by choosing colours that match. The pale blue romper and cardigan for a boy (page 41) could be teamed with a dress and cardigan made with the same materials and embroidery for his elder sister. A four-year-old girl may wear a navy smocked dress whilst her little brother would wear the buster suit with navy button-on pants (page 89). Nanny keeps to the same smocking patterns and shades of embroidery silks as far as possible, as there is enough variety in the mixture of dress and buster suit: anything more would begin to look uncoordinated.

Babies, of course, wear white with colour introduced in the embroidery and when a newborn brother or sister arrives, Nanny will pick out the main colour that her elder charges are wearing to embroider the new baby's outfits. The newborn nightdress, cardigan and bootees embroidered in green (page 12) could be made to match a buster suit with pale green button-on pants and a pale green smocked dress and cardigan.

The combinations are endless but Nanny would always complete the outfits with plain, short, white ankle socks, with matching coloured shoes and Harris tweed coats.

There will always be a demand for bibs and, although towelling is more practical for everyday use, what could be more pretty at a party than these bibs embroidered with the baby's name? This makes it easy for other mothers and nannies instantly to identify the baby. The simple pattern shape makes it a good project for someone who enjoys embroidery more than dressmaking.

PARTY BIB
MATERIALS
30 cm (12 in), white evenweave material (26 threads to 2.5 cm/1 in), 80 cm (32 in) wide
30 cm (12 in), white cotton material or similar for lining, 80 cm (32 in) wide
80 cm (32 in), white bias binding, 13 mm (½ in) wide
1 skein each of embroidery silk in blue, pale blue, flesh, green, dark pink, yellow, beige, brown and white
(girl's bib only) 1.1 metres (1¼ yards) white broderie anglaise edging
(girl's bib only) 1 skein, pink embroidery silk

THE PATTERN

Enlarge the pattern piece given on the right.
Lay the evenweave on top of the lining material and cut out the pattern.
Taking the evenweave and using 2 strands of embroidery silk, work the pattern in cross-stitch and backstitch from the chart, choosing either the girl with balloons on page 52 for a little girl or the elephant design on page 53 for a boy. Work your baby's name using the alphabet chart on page 124.

TO MAKE THE BIB

1. For the girl's bib only:
Pin the broderie anglaise around the seam line of the evenweave material, *right* sides together and so that the raw edges of both are facing outwards. Gather slightly at the corners and leave the neckline free. The raw edges at each end of the broderie anglaise will be covered later. Tack in place.
2. Place the lining material over the evenweave, *right* sides together and stitch 1 cm (⅜ in) in from outside edge, leaving the neckline free.
3. Turn the bib *right* side out through the neck opening. Reshape, pin and press the seams.
4. Pin the bias binding to the neckline, beginning at the centre of both. Stitch in place. Fold the binding over the raw edges of the neckline. Slipstitch to the bib, thus enclosing the raw edges of the broderie anglaise on the girl's bib, then continue up the remainder of the bias on both sides to make the ties, turning in 6 mm (¼ in) at the ends.

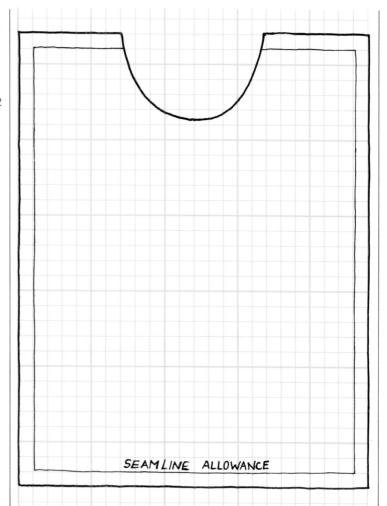

SEAM LINE   ALLOWANCE

BIB PATTERN

*One dot represents one cross stitch; see page 114 for instructions on working
cross stitch. A small section of the border is given at the top right of the chart.
The border is worked all round the straight sides of the bib beginning about
5 mm (³/₁₆ in) in from the sides. Position the rest of the motif centrally between
the base of the neckline and the bottom of the bib. The balloon strings and hair
bows are worked in back stitch.*

One dot represents one cross stitch; see page 114 for instructions on working
cross stitch. Only a corner of the border pattern is shown on the chart (top right).
Work this pattern on all straight sides of the bib beginning about 3 mm (⅛ in)
from the sides. Position the rest of the motif so that the base of the baby's name is
about 35 mm (1⅜ in) from the bottom. The outline of the elephant and the
balloon strings are worked in back stitch.

3 PLY CARDIGAN
SIZE: 6 MONTHS
MATERIALS
40 grams (2 oz) × 3 ply, white wool
scraps of embroidery silks in pale blue, pink,
dark pink and pale green
5 small white buttons with star-shaped cut-out
1 pair each 3¼ mm & 2¾ mm (nos. 10 & 12)
needles

BACK
Using 2¾ mm (no. 12) needles, cast on 69 sts.
Rib 10 rows.
Change to 3¼ mm (no. 10) needles.
Stocking st 34 rows, ending with a purl row.
Cast off 3 sts at the beginning of next two rows.
Next row: k1, sl.1, k1, psso, knit to last 3 sts, k2tog, k1.
Next row: k1, purl to last st, k1.
Repeat last 2 rows until 25 sts remain on needle.
Cast off.

RIGHT FRONT
Using 2¾ mm (no. 12) needles, cast on 39 sts. (This includes 6 sts for the border.)
Rib 2 rows, beginning k2, p1, k1, p1, . . .
Next row: make buttonhole as follows: k2, p1, yfwd, k2tog, rib to end.
Rib 7 more rows.
Change to 3¼ mm (no. 10) needles and work in stocking st with rib border:
Next row: k2, p1, k1, p1, knit to end.
Next row: k1, p33, k1, p1, k1, p1, k1.
Continue for 33 more rows, working buttonholes on rows 1, 11, 23 and 33.
Next row: cast off 3 sts, purl to last 8 sts, p2tog, rib 6.
Next row: rib 6, knit to last 3 sts, k2tog, k1.
Next row: k1, purl to last 6 sts,

rib 6.
Next row: rib 6, knit to last 3 sts, k2tog, k1.
Next row: k1, purl to last 8 sts, p2tog, rib 6.
Repeat last 4 rows until 11 sts remain.
Next row: rib 6, k2, k2tog, k1.
Next row: k1, p3, rib 6.
Next row: rib 6, k1, k2tog, k1.
Next row: k1, p2, rib 6.
Next row: rib 6, k2tog, k1.
Next row: k1, p1, rib 6.
Next row: rib 5, k3tog.
Rib 10 more rows on these 6 sts.
Cast off.

LEFT FRONT
Using 2¾ mm (no. 12) needles, cast on 39 sts. (This includes 6 sts for the border.)
Rib 10 rows, starting k2, p1, k1, p1, . . .
Change to 3¼ mm (no. 10) needles and work in stocking st with rib border.
Next row: k34, p1, k1, p1, k2.
Next row: k1, p1, k1, p1, k1, purl to last st, k1.
Continue for 32 more rows.
Next row: cast off 3 sts, knit to last 8 sts, k2tog, rib 6.
Next row: rib 6, purl to last st, k1.
Next row: k1, k2tog, knit to last 6 sts, rib 6.
Next row: rib 6, purl to last st, k1.
Next row: k1, k2tog, knit to last 8 sts, k2tog, rib 6.
Repeat last 4 rows until 10 sts remain.

Next row: rib 6, p3, k1.
Next row: k1, sl.1, k1, psso, k1, rib 6.
Next row: rib 6, p2, k1.
Next row: k1, sl.1, k1, psso, rib 6.
Next row: rib 6, p1, k1.
Next row: k3tog, rib 5.
Rib 10 more rows on these 6 stitches.
Cast off.

SLEEVES
Using 2¾ mm (no. 12) needles, cast on 33 sts.
Rib 10 rows.
Change to 3¼ mm (no. 10) needles and stocking st 6 rows.
Continue in stocking st, increasing 1 st at each end of next and every 4th row until 51 sts.
Work 5 rows without shaping.
Cast off 3 sts at beginning of next 2 rows.
Next row: k1, sl.1, k1, psso, knit to last 3 sts, k2tog, k1.
Next row: k1, purl to last st, k1.
Repeat last 2 rows until 7 sts remain.
Cast off.

TO MAKE UP

Join the side and sleeve seams and stitch the sleeves into position. Join the ends of the neckband and stitch into position round the back of the neck.

Attach the buttons to correspond with buttonholes, using 3 strands of embroidery silk to sew 2 french knots in the middle of the buttons, one pink and one blue. Using 3 strands of embroidery silk, work embroidery as indicated in the diagram on the left, making pink rosebuds with blue french knots for a girl or blue rosebuds with pink french knots for a boy.

Alternatively, the cardigan may be trimmed with ribbons and lace instead of embroidery. Choose a lace insertion with eyelets. Thread with a ribbon to match the dress or romper and sew round the cardigan border, as shown in the diagram on the right, turning under the raw edges.

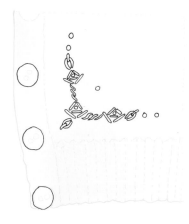

BOOTEES

SIZE: 6 MONTHS

MATERIALS

20 grams (1 oz) × 4 ply, white wool
1 metre (1 yard), white satin ribbon, 6 mm
(¼ in) wide
scraps of embroidery silk in pale blue, pink and
dark pink
1 pair 3¾ mm (no. 9) needles

Cast on 29 sts.
Rib 4 rows.
Stocking st 10 rows.
Row 1: k1, * yfwd, k2tog, repeat from * to end of row.
Row 2: k1, purl to last st, k1.
Row 3: k20, turn,
Row 4: p11, turn,
Stocking st 18 rows on these 11 sts.
Break off yarn.
With right side of work facing, commencing where sts were left and using same needle, knit up 12 sts along side of instep, knit 11 sts on needle, knit up 12 sts along other side of instep, knit remaining 9 sts on left-hand needle. (53 sts.)
Knit 10 rows.

SHAPING FOOT

Row 1: k1, k2tog, k22, [(k2tog) twice], k21, k2tog, k1.
Row 2: knit.
Row 3: k1, k2tog, k20, [(k2tog) twice], k19, k2tog, k1.
Cast off.

TO MAKE UP

Sew the back and foot seams together.
Using 3 strands of embroidery silk, work rosebuds in the centre of each foot to match the cardigan.
Cut the white satin ribbon in half and thread through the eyelets of each bootee.

NINE MONTHS

Snug pyjama suit (see page 58) with scolloping and appliquéed elephant for a 9 month old baby.

NINE MONTHS

At nine months old, baby is growing up and often crawls out of his bedclothes at night time. Something warm to wear is needed, so Nanny bridges the gap between nightgown and pyjamas with a pyjama suit. The suit is very practical as well as attractive, since the buttoned back flap means that it is easy to change the baby but, when this is fastened, he is prevented from undressing himself before he falls asleep and therefore he does not become chilled.

An appliqué animal which adds interest and will be enjoyed by baby is stitched to the front. The animal in the pattern shown on page 56 is made from a remnant of material, however, appliquéed animals can be purchased from main stores and it is then a simple matter to stitch one of these to the front. The collar and cuffs at the wrists and ankles are scolloped to give a dainty finish to the garment.

PYJAMA SUIT

SIZE: 9 MONTHS

MATERIALS

1.3 metres (1½ yards), lemon Viyella,
flannelette or similar material, 90 cm (36 in)
wide or 1.1 metres (1⅙ yards) × 115 cm
(45 in)
70 cm (28 in) narrow elastic, 6 mm (¼ in) wide
1.5 metres (1½ yards) seam binding, 13 mm
(½ in) wide
9 small lemon buttons
1 small press-stud, size 00
2 skeins, pale green embroidery silk
scrap of contrasting material

THE PATTERN

Enlarge the pattern pieces given on pages 61, 62 and 63. Following the diagrams on page 59, lay and cut out the pattern, including a 3 × 36 cm (1¼ × 14¼ in) bias strip for the collar binding. Mark all dots and buttonholes with tailor's tacks. Cut the appliqué pattern on page 60 out in contrasting material. Using a pencil, trace the stitch lines of the elephant on to the appliqué material.

THE SCOLLOPING

1. Mark the scollops on to the collars, wrists and ankles. Embroider with 2 strands of pale green silk, using the method described in the techniques section, page 116.

TO MAKE THE SUIT

JOINING THE FRONT AND THE BACKS

2. Align the 2 front pieces down the centre and join with a french seam. Press.
3. Join the front and shirt backs at the shoulders with a french seam. Press.
4. Make a narrow 6 mm (¼ in) hem across the bottom of the shirt back.
5. Beginning at the armhole, stitch the side seams of the shirt back and front down to the placket with a plain seam. Neaten the edges of the seam with machine whipping, or by hand with blanket stitch. Press.
6. Turn a narrow 6 mm (¼ in) hem down remainder of the shirt back sides.

7. Using a french seam, join the back flap down the centre. Press.
8. Join the side seams of the back and front legs, with a french seam, from the placket downwards. Press.
9. Pin the seam binding across the legs on the line indicated for the elastic casing on the pattern. Stitch both edges of binding in place. Cut 2 pieces of elastic 15 cm (6 in) long, adjusting here if necessary to the size of the baby's ankle plus 2 cm (¾ in) and slot through the binding on each leg. Hold in place at each end with a stitch.
10. Join the centre of the front and back legs with a french seam, thus securing the elastic at the same time. Press.
11. Press in the placket and turn under the small allowance. Stitch

in place by machine or by hand.

THE SLEEVES

12. Make the elastic casings across the sleeves on the line indicated on the pattern, by stitching both edges of the binding. Cut 2 pieces of elastic 15 cm (6 in) long, adjusting here if necessary to the size of the baby's wrist plus 2 cm (¾ in), and slot through the binding on each arm and hold in place at each end with a stitch.

13. Join the side edges of the sleeve with a french seam, thus securing the elastic at the same time.

14. With the pyjama shirt inside out and with *right* sides together,

align the side seams of the sleeve with the side seams of the body. Pin in place. Align the centre dot of the sleeve with the shoulder seam of the body and pin in place.

15. Beginning at the bottom seam of the armhole again, pin up the edges of the armhole until the centre dot has almost been reached. At both sides of the centre dot fold the excess material into a small tuck towards the centre (making a box pleat on the right side). Pin in place.

16. Tack around the armhole, then stitch the seam. Press away from the sleeve. Neaten the edges of the armhole seam with machine whipping, or by hand with blanket stitch.

THE NECKLINE

17. Neaten the shirt buttonband edges if the selvage has not been used.

18. Turn under the shirt buttonband allowance and topstitch as close to the edge as possible.

19. Place the collar, *wrong* side down, on to the *right* side of the pyjama body and matching centre dots. Pin and tack in place around the neckline.

20. With *right* sides together, pin the bias strip to the neck edge of the collar, so that 13 mm (½ in) extends beyond the folded back shirt edge. Stitch in place. Trim the seam.

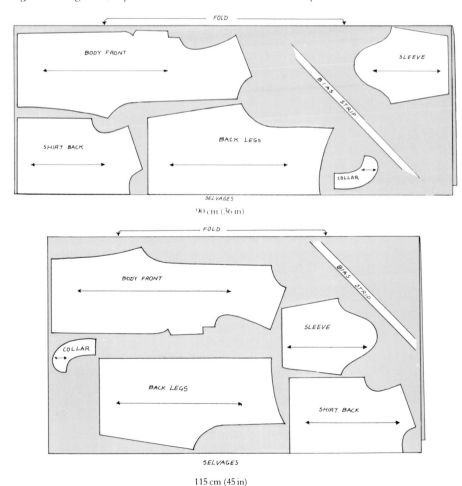

90 cm (36 in)

115 cm (45 in)

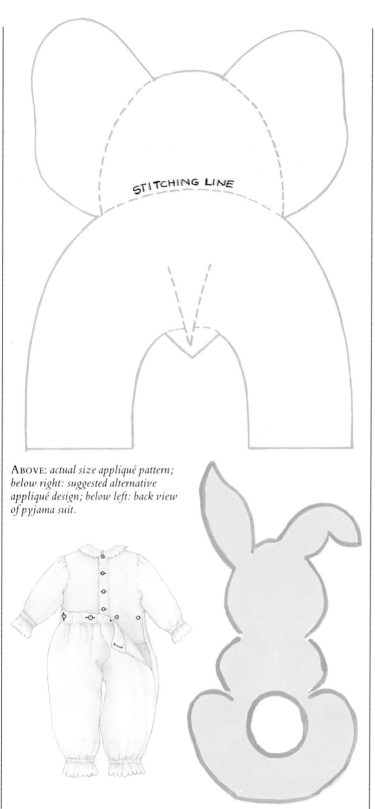

STITCHING LINE

ABOVE: *actual size appliqué pattern; below right: suggested alternative appliqué design; below left: back view of pyjama suit.*

21. Turn the bias strip completely over to the inside of the pyjama neckline. Turn in the lower edge of the bias and slipstitch in place, also turning in the ends at the back.

FINISHING THE BACK
22. Make buttonholes down the back in the positions shown on the pattern. Using 3 strands of pale green embroidery silk, sew the buttons in position with 2 downward stitches.
23. Turn in 6 mm (¼ in) along the top of the back flap. Turn in another 2.5 cm (1 in) to make a wide casing and stitch in place.
24. Make buttonholes along this band in the positions shown on the pattern. Slot 32 cm (12½ in) of the elastic through the casing underneath the buttonholes. Secure at each end with a few stitches.
25. Turn in the seam allowance along the side edges of the back flap and stitch in place.
26. Sew the buttons for the back flap on to the shirt back in the positions shown on the pattern, using 3 strands of embroidery silk as before.
27. Sew the press-stud at the back of the neck.

THE ELEPHANT

28. Loosely tack the elephant in place on the centre front of the body. Stitch it in place with a zig-zag stitch on the machine, or by hand with buttonhole stitch.
29. Using 2 strands of embroidery silk, work the stitch lines of the elephant with stem stitch or buttonhole stitch.

PYJAMA SUIT N.B. Seam allowance = 1 cm (⅜ in)

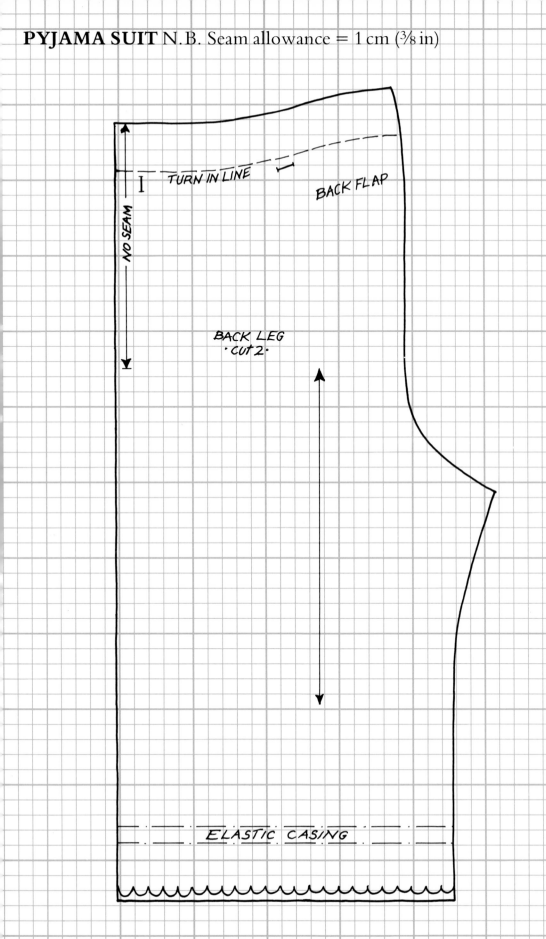

NO SEAM

TURN IN LINE

BACK FLAP

BACK LEG
· CUT 2 ·

ELASTIC CASING

PYJAMA SUIT

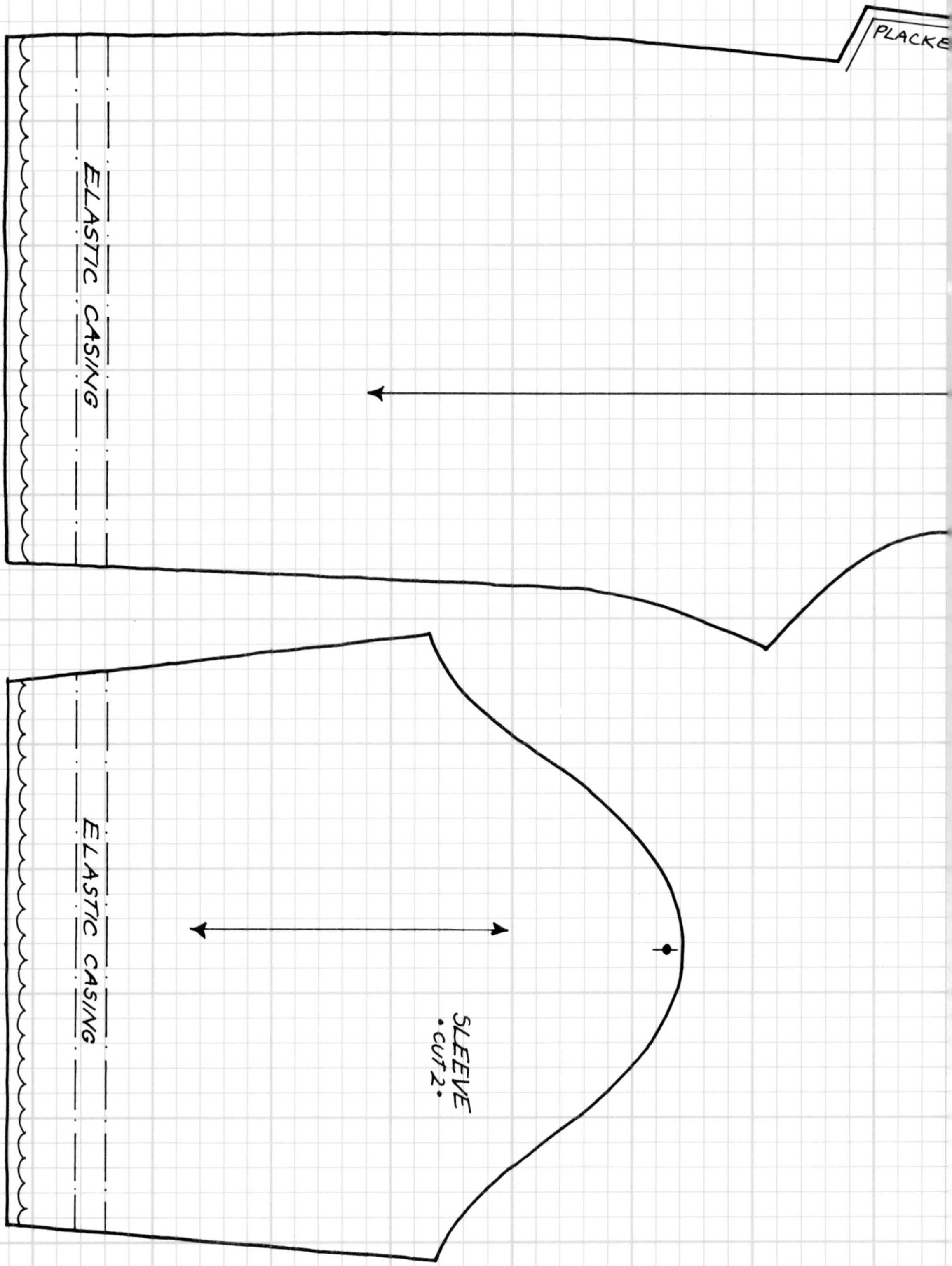

ELASTIC CASING

PLACKE

ELASTIC CASING

SLEEVE
· CUT 2 ·

62

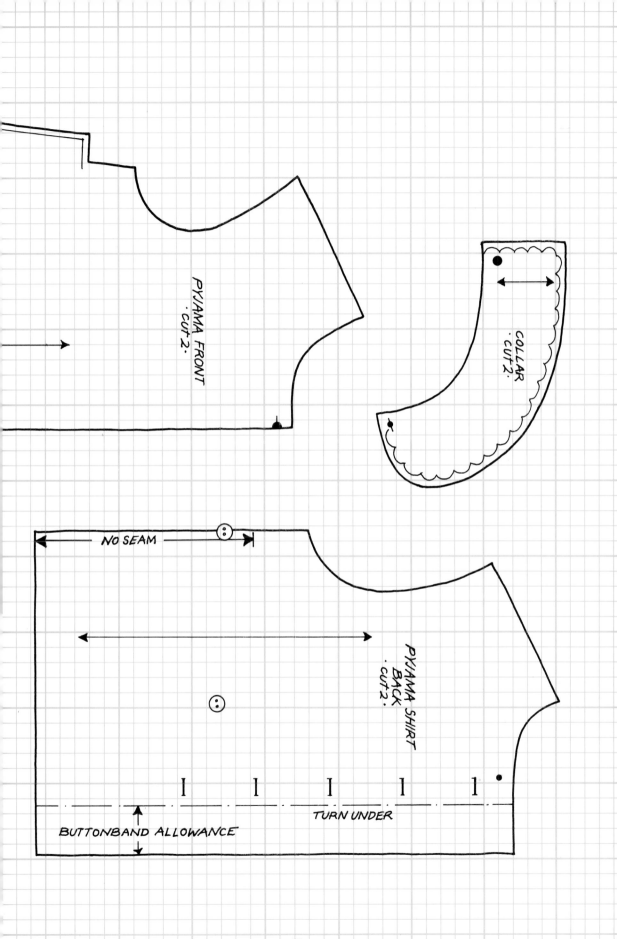

PYJAMA FRONT
·CUT·2·

COLLAR
·CUT·2·

NO SEAM

PYJAMA SHIRT
BACK
·CUT·2·

TURN UNDER

BUTTONBAND ALLOWANCE

TWELVE MONTHS

Smocked dress (page 66) and matching cardigan (page 70) for a 12 month old girl with romper suit (page 69) for a boy of the same age.

TWELVE MONTHS

Smocked dresses on a yoke are very popular, as well as being a classic design. Nanny continues to make them for her charges as they are so flattering to the 'chubby tummy' shape of this age group. She will add variety to the wardrobe by embroidering the garments with smocking in different lengths, some only a few rows and others to the waist, but always at the front and the back. Materials chosen now include pinstripes, tiny checks or spots, while white is kept for parties and special occasions. Brighter colours, such as reds and navies may be introduced but only in the form of trimmings or embroidery, as it is traditionally felt that these colours tend to overpower the small toddler.

No matter what the occasion, whether a special one or just a normal day, a little girl will wear a petticoat under her dress. Nanny may use tucks, another traditional method of allowing room for growth, and the petticoat will always be white, trimmed with a colour taken from the dress it is to be worn with.

Boys are beginning to wear shirts with button-on pants but romper suits are still part of their wardrobe and the more usual choice for a party. Cardigans team with the outfit and may be decorated with lace, even for a boy.

Shoes are not worn at this age even if baby is beginning to walk. White socks may be worn in the winter and Nanny ensures that these are ankle length and plain knit, rather than patterned. Traditionally, woollen tights are not worn even in the coldest weather.

The romper and dress shown here are still smocked with basic stitches and so are not complicated to embroider. The scolloping in this dress is varied by the use of contrasting materials. The petticoat has tucks, which can be let down as the toddler grows, and has a pocket complete with matching handkerchief. It is designed with a narrow bodice, so that most of the material is used in the skirt, giving greater fullness to the dress it is worn under. The cardigan is embroidered on the front, back and sleeves to match the dress, but would be equally suitable for a boy if his romper suit were made in pale blue like the one given in the six-month section on page 38.

SMOCKED DRESS
SIZE: 12 MONTHS
MATERIALS

1.5 metres (1½ yards), pale blue with white spot Viyella, Clydella or similar, 90 cm (36 in) wide or 1.2 metres (1¼ yards) × 115 (45 in) wide

0.25 metre (¼ yard), white Viyella, Clydella or similar, 90 cm (36 in) or 115 cm (45 in) wide

50 cm (½ yard), white cotton lace edging, 13 mm (½ in) wide

1 skein, blue embroidery silk

2 skeins, white embroidery silk

5 small white buttons

1 small press-stud, size 00

THE PATTERN
Enlarge the pattern pieces given on pages 77, 78 and 79. Following the diagrams on page 67, lay and cut out the pattern, including a 3 × 36 cm (1¼ × 14¼ in) bias strip for the binding around the neckline. Cut the cuffs out in the white material or as shown if not using contrasting material. Mark all dots, crosses and buttonholes with tailor's tacks.

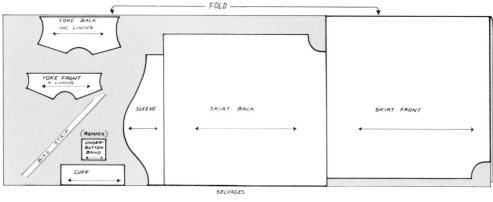

90 cm (36 in)

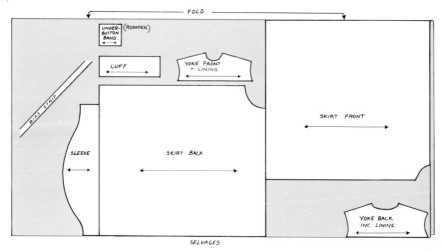

115 cm (45 in)

THE SMOCKING AND THE SCOLLOPING

1. Following the smocking instructions, page 116, make 18 rows of gathering on the front skirt and 13 rows on the skirt backs. Pull up the gathering until the material is slightly narrower than the corresponding yoke. Using 2 strands of white embroidery silk, smock pattern D across the gathering. Smock the shortened version on the backs (rows 5 to 15 inclusive, beginning on the second row of the guide threads).

2. Mark the scollops on to the cuffs and embroider with 2 strands of blue silk, as described in the techniques section, page 116.

Do not embroider the french knots yet.

TO MAKE THE DRESS

JOINING THE YOKES AND SKIRTS

3. Place the *right* sides of the front yoke and the front skirt together, matching centre dots. Pin the top edge of the smocking to the lower edge of the yoke, spreading the fullness evenly. Tack in place, then stitch across the seam. Press the seam towards the yoke.

4. With *right* sides together, align the left back yoke with the left back skirt. Pin the top edge of the smocking to the lower edge of the yoke, spreading the fullness evenly. Make sure that the centre dots are matching and allow the yoke lining to extend beyond the skirt edge. Tack in place, then stitch across the seam. Press the seam towards the yoke.

5. Repeat the procedure with the right back yoke and skirt.

6. Remove all the guide threads from the smocking.

7. Join the front and back yokes at the shoulders, *right* sides together, with a plain seam, leaving the lining of the back yokes hanging free. Press the seam open.

8. Using a plain seam, join the back skirts along the selvage, from the hem to point C on the pattern. Press the seam open.

9. Using a french seam join the side seams of the front and back skirts. Press.

THE SLEEVES

10. Make 2 rows of hand or machine gathering stitches between the crosses on the top and bottom edges of the sleeve, as marked on the pattern.

11. Pull up the gathers on the lower edge of the sleeve until it is the same length as the cuff. Spread the gathers evenly.

12. Join the side edges of the sleeve with a french seam and the side edges of the cuffs with a plain seam.

13. Pin the *right* side of the cuff to the *wrong* side of the sleeve, matching the centre dots, side seams and raw edges. Spread the gathers evenly and stitch around the seam. Press cuff away from sleeve.

14. Fold the cuff over to the *right* side of the sleeve along the fold line. Press. Pin the scolloping over the seam line. Using 2 strands of blue embroidery silk, sew in place with a french knot in the middle of each scollop. The cuff should now be approximately 2.5 cm (1 in) wide.

15. Turn the dress inside out and, with *right* sides together, align the side seams of the sleeve with the side seams of the skirt. Pin in place, continue up the edges of the armhole until the gathering stitches are reached. Align the centre dot of the sleeve with the shoulder seam of the yoke and pin in place. Pull up the gathers until the sleeve fits the armhole and pin. Tack, then stitch the seam.

16. Remove the gathering threads. Press the seam away from sleeve. Neaten the lower edges of the armhole seam, between the front and back yokes.

THE LINING

17. Join the back yoke lining to the front yoke lining at the shoulders, *right* sides together, with a plain seam. Press the seam open.

18. Fold the lining over and with *wrong* sides together, pin, then tack the yoke lining to the yoke around the neckline, aligning the corresponding shoulder seams.

19. On the inside, turn under the seam allowances on the front and back yoke lining. Press the yoke/sleeve seams inwards and pin the lining over this and the yoke/skirt seams. Slipstitch in place (thus enclosing all raw edges).

THE NECKLINE

20. With *right* sides together, pin the bias strip to the yoke neckline, turning in 1 cm (⅜ in) at each end. Stitch in place.

21. Trim the seam allowances, then fold the binding up over them to the inside of the yoke. Turn under the remaining edge of the strip and pin to the seam line. Slipstitch in place.

22. Gather the lace and stitch it around the neckline where the binding joins the yoke.

THE HEM AND BACK

23. Turn under 5 cm (2 in) along the bottom edge of the skirt. Turn up another 6 cm (2⅜ in) to make a double hem. Adjust here according to the child's height. Slipstitch in place.

24. Make buttonholes down the back in the position shown on the pattern. Using 3 strands of blue embroidery silk, sew buttons in position with 2 french knots. This makes a small fold in the skirt when the buttons are fastened.

25. Sew a small press-stud on to the neck bias.

SMOCKING PATTERN D: *work rows 5 to 15 only on backs.*

SMOCKED ROMPER

SIZE: 12 MONTHS

MATERIALS

*1.3 metres (1½ yards) polyester cotton satin
stripe or similar, 90 cm (36 in) wide or 1.1
metres (1¼ yards) × 115 cm (45 in)
40 cm (16 in), elastic, 6 mm (¼ in) wide
3 skeins, red embroidery silk
10 small white buttons, with star-shaped cut-
out, and 2 plain white buttons
1 small press-stud, size 00*

THE PATTERN

Enlarge the pattern pieces given
on pages 77, 78 and 79. Lay and
cut out the pattern, as for the
dress, using the correct cuff
pattern and cutting line on the
skirt and cutting out the under-
buttonband. Include a 3 × 36 cm
(1¼ × 14¼ in) bias strip for the
binding around the neckline.
Mark all dots and buttonholes
with tailor's tacks.

THE SMOCKING

1. Following the smocking
instructions, page 116, make 21
rows of gathering on the front
skirt and 17 rows on the skirt
backs. Pull up the gathering until
the material is slightly narrower
than the corresponding yoke.
Using 2 strands of red embroidery
silk, smock pattern E across the
gathering. Smock the shortened
version on the backs (17 rows).

TO MAKE THE ROMPER

2. Follow the instructions for the
Smocked Romper, page 38, from
step 3 to step 31 inclusive. The
cuff will be wide enough to turn
back. Make buttonholes and use
red silk to sew on the buttons.
3. Using 2 strands of embroidery
silk, stitch small bullion knots
round the cuffs and neck binding.
4. Sew press-stud on neck bias.

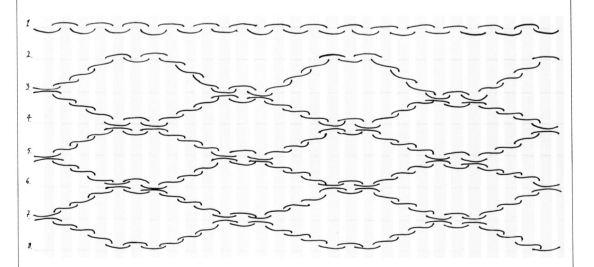

SMOCKING PATTERN E: *work to
row 21 on front and row 17 on backs.*

3 PLY CARDIGAN
SIZE: 12 MONTHS
MATERIALS

50 grams (2½ oz) × 3 ply, white wool
1 skein, pale blue embroidery silk
1 skein, blue embroidery silk
1 skein, pale green embroidery silk
1 metre (1 yard), pale blue satin ribbon, 6 mm (¼ in) wide
1 metre (1 yard), white cotton lace edging, 1.5 cm (⅝ in) wide
5 small white buttons with star-shaped cut-out
1 pair each 3¼ mm & 2¾ mm (nos. 10 & 12) needles

BACK

Using 2¾ mm (no. 12) needles, cast on 70 sts.
Rib 6 rows starting with k1, p1, . . .
Next row: k1, * yfwd, k2tog, rib 4, k2tog, yrn, p1, k1, repeat from * to last 9 sts, yfwd, k2tog, rib 3, k2tog, yfwd, k2.
Rib 5 more rows.
Change to 3¼ mm (no. 10) needles.
Stocking st 40 rows, ending with a purl row.
Cast off 3 sts at beginning of next 2 rows.
Next row: k1, sl.1, k1, psso, knit to last 3 sts, k2tog, k1.
Next row: k1, purl to last st, k1.
Repeat last 2 rows until 20 sts remain, ending with a purl row.
Cast off.

RIGHT FRONT

Using 2¾ mm (no. 12) needles, cast on 40 sts. (This includes 6 sts for the buttonband.)
Rib 2 rows, beginning k2, p1, k1, p1, . . .
Next row: make buttonhole as follows: k2, p1, yrn, p2tog, rib to end.
Rib 3 rows.
Next row: k2, p1, k1, p1, k1, [(k2tog, yrn, rib 2, yfwd, k2tog, rib 4), 3 times], k2tog, yrn,

p1, k1.
Rib 5 more rows.
Change to 3¼ mm (no. 10) needles and work in stocking st with rib border as follows:
Next row: k2, p1, k1, p1, knit to end.
Next row: k1, purl to last 6 sts, rib 6.
Continue in stocking st with rib border for 39 more rows, working buttonholes as before on rows 1, 13, 25 and 37.
Next row: cast off 3 sts, purl to last 8 sts, p2tog tb1, rib 6.
Next row: rib 6, knit to last 3 sts, k2tog, k1.
Next row: k1, purl to last 6 sts, rib 6.
Next row: rib 6, knit to last 3 sts, k2tog, k1.
Next row: k1, purl to last 6 sts, rib 6.
Next row: rib 6, k2tog tb1, knit to last 3 sts, k2tog, k1.
Continue, decreasing 1 st at front edge inside rib border on every following 5th row, *at the same time* decreasing at raglan edge on alt. rows until 16 sts remain.
Dec. 1 st at raglan edge only on every alt. row until 8 sts remain.
Rib 5, k3tog.
Continue to rib on these 6 sts for 13 more rows.
Cast off.

LEFT FRONT

Using 2¾ mm (no. 12) needles, cast on 40 sts. (This includes 6 sts for the buttonband.)
Rib 6 rows, starting k1, p1, k1, p1, . . .
Next row: rib 2, [(yfwd, k2tog, rib 4, k2tog, yfwd, rib 2), 3 times], yfwd, k2tog, rib 6.
Rib 5 more rows.
Change to 3¼ mm (no. 10) needles and work in stocking st with rib border as follows:
Next row: knit to last 6 sts, rib 6.
Next row: rib 6, purl to last st, k1.
Continue in stocking st with rib border for 38 more rows.
Next row: cast off 3 sts, knit to last 8 sts, k2tog, rib 6.
Next row: rib 6, purl to last st, k1.
Next row: k1, sl.1, k1, psso, knit to last 6 sts, rib 6.
Next row: rib 6, purl to last st, k1.
Next row: k1, sl.1, k1, psso, knit to last 6 sts, rib 6.
Next row: rib 6, p2tog, purl to last st, k1.
Continue, decreasing 1 st at front edge inside rib border on every following 5th row, *at the same time* decreasing at the raglan edge on knit rows, until 16 sts remain.
Dec. 1 st at raglan edge on knit rows only until 8 sts remain.

Next row: k3tog tb1, rib to end.
Continue to rib on these 6 sts for
13 more rows.
Cast off.

SLEEVES

Using 2¾ mm (no. 12) needles,
cast on 36 sts.
Rib 11 rows.
Next row: rib 3, [(inc. in next st,
rib 3), 7 times], inc. in next st, rib
to end. (44 sts.)
Change to 3¼ mm (no. 10)
needles and continue in stocking
st, increasing in first and last stitch
on 3rd and every following 6th
row until 54 sts.
Continue on these sts without
increasing for 21 rows.
Cast off 3 sts at beginning of next
2 rows.
Next row: k1, sl.1, k1, psso, knit
to last 3 sts, k2tog, k1.
Next row: k1, purl to last st, k1.
Repeat last 2 rows until 6 sts
remain ending with a purl row.
Cast off.

TO MAKE UP

Join the side and sleeve seams and
stitch into position. Join the ends
of the neckband and stitch into
position round the back of the
neck.
Attach the buttons to correspond
with buttonholes. Use 3 strands
of embroidery silk to sew 2 french
knots in the buttons.
Beginning centre back, sew the
lace to the edges of the body,
gathering it slightly round the
corners of the buttonbands.
Beginning at the front after the
second hole, work pale blue
rosebuds with blue centres and
pale green leaves in alternate gaps
between the eyelet holes in the
ribbing. Thread the satin ribbon
through the eyelets, so that the
rosebuds are not covered.
Work rosebuds in the centre of the
back neckband and in the centre of
the cuffs.

THE PETTICOAT
Size: 12 months
MATERIALS

*1.2 metres (1¼ yards), white cotton lawn,
polyester cotton or similar, 90 cm (36 in) wide
or 1 metre (1 yard) × 115 cm (45 in)
2 metres (2 yards), white satin ribbon, 6 mm
(¼ in) wide
1.6 metres (1¾ yards), white lace eyelet
insertion, 1.5 cm (⅝ in) wide
2.5 metres (2½ yards), pale blue satin ribbon,
6 mm (¼ in) wide
3 metres (3 yards), white lace edging, 1 cm
(⅜ in) wide
1 small white button*

THE PATTERN

Enlarge the pattern pieces given
on pages 74 and 75.
Following the diagrams on page
76, lay and cut out the pattern,
including one 3.5 × 57 cm (1⅜ in
× 23½ in) bias strip (this may
need to be cut in 2 pieces and
joined) and one 3 × 25 cm (1¼ ×
10 in) bias strip.
Mark all dots, crosses and
buttonholes with tailor's tacks.

TO MAKE THE PETTICOAT

The skirt

1. Join the skirt backs to the front
at the side edges with french
seams. Press.
2. Beginning with the bottom
tuck, fold the skirt along the
lower line right across the skirt
front and backs. Press the fold and
stitch 1 cm (⅜ in) from the edge of
the fold. Press the tuck
downwards and repeat the
procedure along the other 2 fold
lines.
3. Make 2 rows of hand or
machine gathering stitches
between the crosses at the top
edge of the skirt, as marked on the
pattern.

4. Neaten the side edges of the
centre back with a very tiny 3 mm
(⅛ in) hem for 5 cm (2 in) down
from the top edge.

The pocket

NB The seam allowance on the
sides and bottom of the pocket is
only 6 mm (¼ in). The top edge is
the usual 1 cm (⅜ in).
5. Turn down and press the seam
allowance along the top of the
pocket. Sew 8 cm (3¼ in) of the
lace edging along the fold, so that
lace extends upwards.
6. Turn in and press the seam
allowances on the sides and
bottom. With the *wrong* side of
the pocket against the *right* side of
the skirt pin in position aligning
dots and topstitch along sides and
bottom as close to the edges of the
pocket as possible.

Joining the skirt to the top

7. Join the bodice at the shoulders
with a french seam. Press.
8. Using a french seam, join the
side edges of the bodice. Press.
9. Taking the skirt, pull up the
gathers to roughly the same size as
the lower edge of the bodice.
10. With *right* sides together, pin
the top edge of the skirt to the

Petticoat complete with handkerchief (see page 71) for a 12 month old girl, trimmed to match the dress on page 66.

lower edge of the bodice. Spread the gathers evenly and so that the centre dot and side seams of the skirt match the centre dot and armhole seams of the bodice. Tack, then stitch. Press seam towards bodice.

11. Turn in 1.5 cm (⅝ in) down each centre back edge of the bodice and topstitch as close to the folded edge as possible. (This will also turn in the neatened edge of the skirt.)

12. With the *wrong* side of the skirt and the *right* side of the 3.5 cm (1⅜ in) wide bias binding together, align the stitching line at the top of the bias along the waist seam just made. Pin through all 3 layers and stitch.

13. Fold the bias binding upwards, away from the skirt. Turn in the seam allowance on the other edge of the bias and turn in the side edges. Pin to the bodice. Topstitch along this folded edge (thus enclosing the raw edges). Leave open at the sides for the ribbon (see step 25).

14. Join the centre back seam of the skirt with a french seam. Begin at the hem edge and continue the seam to 6 mm (¼ in) over the neatened edge.

THE BODICE

15. With *right* sides together, pin the other bias strip to the neckline, so that at least 13 mm (½ in) extends beyond the bodice centre back edge at both ends. Stitch in place.

16. Turn the bias strip completely over to the inside of the neckline and folding in the seam allowance, slipstitch the lower fold of the bias in place, turning in the ends at the side edge but

leaving open the sides for the ribbon (see step 25).

17. Make a very tiny 3 mm (⅛ in) hem round the armholes, topstitching in place. This is usually easier to do by hand.

18. Make a buttonhole on the bodice back in the position shown on the pattern. Sew button in corresponding position on other bodice back.

TRIMMING THE PETTICOAT

19. Make a narrow 6 mm (¼ in) hem along the bottom of the skirt. Topstitch in place.

20. Pin and topstitch the lace edging round the hemline of the skirt.

21. Pin and topstitch the lace edging around the 2 armhole edges. (Again this is easier done by hand.)

22. Thread the pale blue ribbon through the eyelets in the lace insertion. Cut off the extra ribbon.

23. Pin the lace insertion centrally between the hem and the lowest tuck turning in the raw edges. Topstitch both edges of the lace insertion in place.

24. Make 3 small bows with the pale blue ribbon and sew 2 on the lace insertion and one on the pocket in the positions illustrated.

25. Thread 1 metre (1 yard) of the white satin ribbon through the waistband and 1 metre (1 yard) through the bias binding at the neckline.

THE HANDKERCHIEF

26. Turn a tiny hem all round the edges of the handkerchief. Topstitch the lace edging to the hems.

Sew a bow made from the pale blue ribbon to one corner.

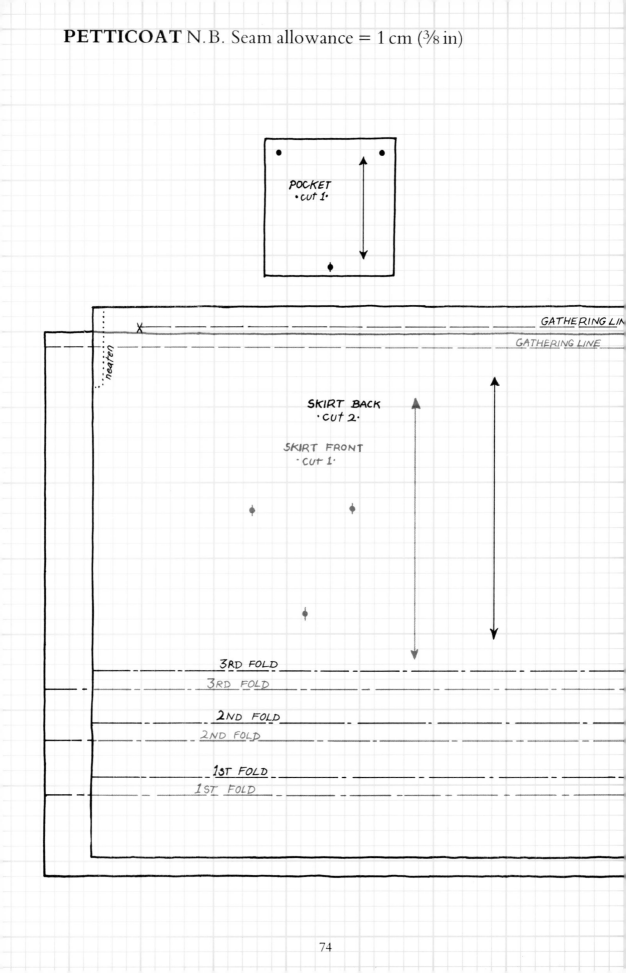

POCKET
· cut 1·

GATHERING LINE

GATHERING LINE

neaten

SKIRT BACK
· cut 2·

SKIRT FRONT
· cut 1·

3RD FOLD

3RD FOLD

2ND FOLD

2ND FOLD

1ST FOLD

1ST FOLD

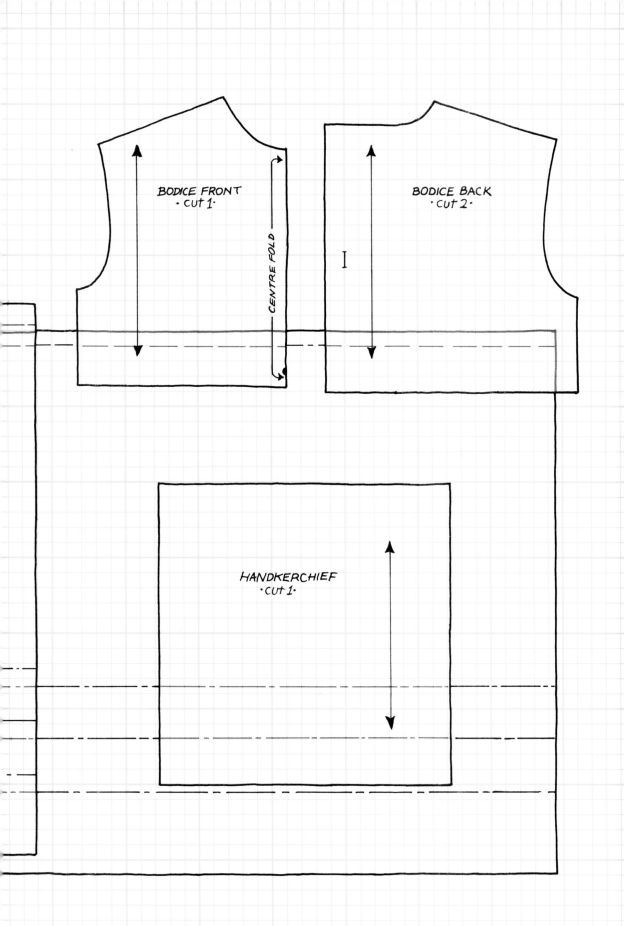

BODICE FRONT
· cut 1·

BODICE BACK
· cut 2·

CENTRE FOLD

HANDKERCHIEF
· cut 1·

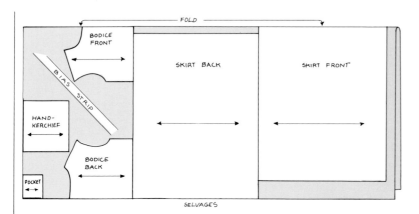

90 cm (36 in)

TWO ALTERNATIVE TRIMMINGS

1. BRODERIE ANGLAISE

Follow steps 1 to 18, then:
19. Make a narrow 6 mm (¼ in) hem along the bottom of the skirt. Topstitch in place.
20. Pin and topstitch broderie anglaise edging around the hemline of the skirt.
21. Pin and topstitch broderie anglaise edging round the 2 armhole edges. (Again this is easier done by hand.)
22. Leaving 6 mm (¼ in) free at each end of the broderie anglaise eyelet insertion, thread 1 metre (1 yard) of coloured satin ribbon through the eyelets. Divide it to hang equally at each end.
23. Pin the broderie anglaise eyelet insertion to the waistband, turning in 6 mm (¼ in) at each end and beginning at the skirt centre back edge. Topstitch both edges.
24. Using 53 cm (22 in) of the same coloured satin ribbon, make a bow in the middle. Stitch to the centre front of the eyelet insertion, so that the long ends hang free.
25. Thread 1 metre (1 yard) of the same ribbon through the bias binding at the neckline.
26. Make the handkerchief as described in the main pattern and trim with broderie anglaise edging.

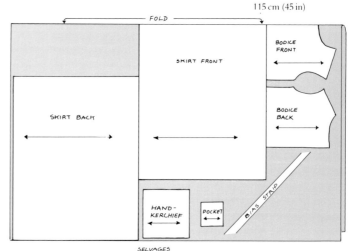

115 cm (45 in)

2. ROSEBUD EMBROIDERY

Follow steps 1 to 7 but work step 2 as follows:
2. Taking the skirt, make a proper hem, so that the finished length of the piece is 26 cm (10½ in). Make two pintucks, 1.5 cm (⅝ in) apart and 1 cm (⅜ in) above the hem stitching. Before working step 8, find the centre of both shoulder seams. Make two pintucks, 1.5 cm (⅝ in) apart, on either side of these points, running down the front and the back bodice to the waistline. Continue with steps 8 to 18 inclusive.
19. Thread 1 metre (1 yard) of white satin ribbon through the waistband and 1 metre (1 yard) through the bias binding at the neckline.
20. Embroider the rosebud pattern (page 85) between the pintucks round the skirt and down the bodice, as shown in the diagram.

12 MONTH DRESS & ROMPER SUIT N.B. Seam allowance = 1 cm (⅜ in)

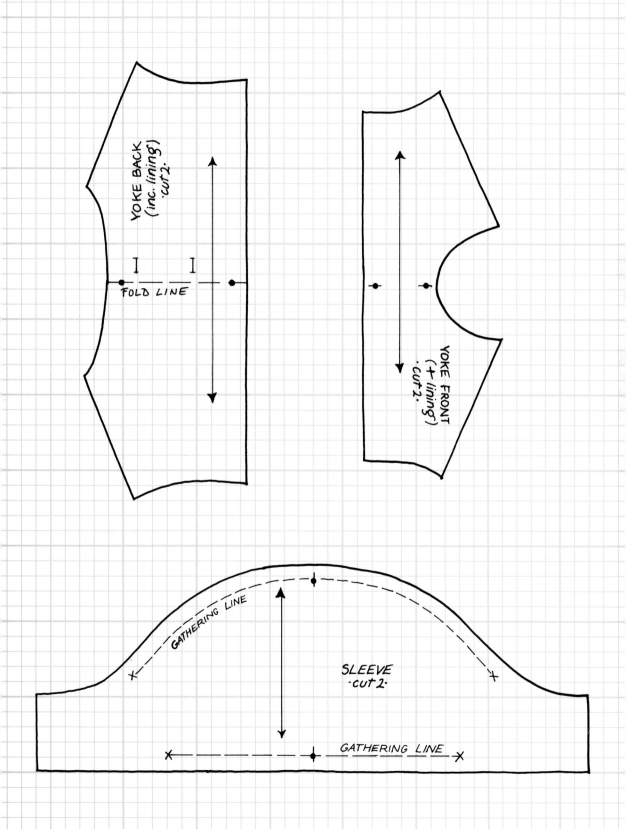

YOKE BACK (inc. lining) ·cut 2·

FOLD LINE

YOKE FRONT (+ lining) ·cut 2·

GATHERING LINE

SLEEVE ·cut 2·

GATHERING LINE

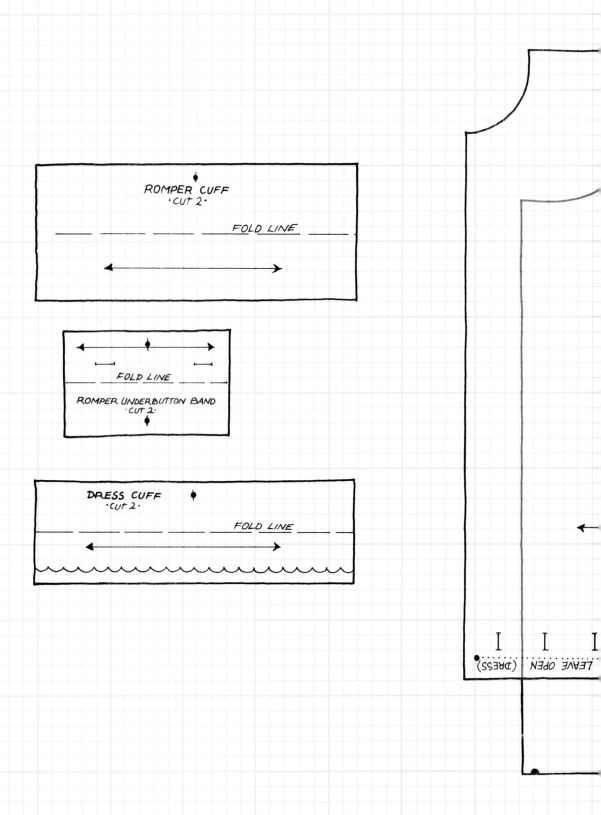

ROMPER CUFF
·CUT 2·

FOLD LINE

FOLD LINE

ROMPER UNDERBUTTON BAND
·CUT 2·

DRESS CUFF
·CUT 2·

FOLD LINE

LEAVE OPEN (DRESS)

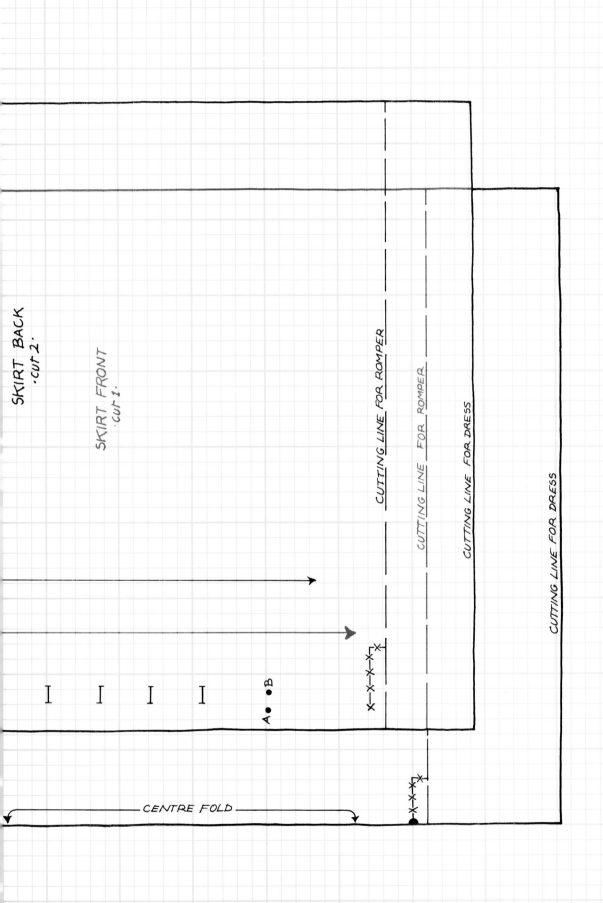

SKIRT BACK
·cut 2·

SKIRT FRONT
·cut 1·

CUTTING LINE FOR ROMPER

CUTTING LINE FOR ROMPER

CUTTING LINE FOR DRESS

CUTTING LINE FOR DRESS

A● ●B

CENTRE FOLD

EIGHTEEN MONTHS

Apricot patterned dress (see page 84) for an 18 month old, teamed with a crossover cardigan (page 82), embroidered to match.

EIGHTEEN MONTHS

Dresses for girls do not change very much but Nanny ensures that at eighteen months they have deep hems, since her charges grow little widthways at this stage and therefore dresses can go on for years provided they are just let down. A smart dress one year will become second best the following, then will be worn for everyday playing for another two years. Little girls will not wear trousers except when going to play outside in the winter and for this the trousers will need to be roomy enough to go over the top of the dress.

Shoes, which are worn now, will be plain and fasten with a bar across the foot, not round the ankle. They used to be fastened with a button but this style is now almost impossible to buy. As shoes are outgrown so quickly, it is not normally possible to have a pair to match every outfit. Nanny will try to choose a colour that will tone with most garments, for example, brown would not be worn with a navy outfit but red shoes would be permissible if the navy garment were trimmed with red.

The ruffle which trims the dress shown in the photograph on page 80 is an easy alternative for people who have difficulty in obtaining the right kind of lace, as it can be made from spare scraps of plain material. The cross-over cardigan is a classic style and could even be embroidered for a boy, in colours to tone with his buster suit.

CROSSOVER CARDIGAN
SIZE: 18 MONTHS
MATERIALS
50 grams (2½ oz) × 2 ply, white wool
1 skein, pale green embroidery silk
1 skein, apricot embroidery silk
1 skein, pale apricot embroidery silk
4 small white buttons with star-shaped cut-out
1 pair each 2¾ mm & 3 mm (nos. 12 & 11)
needles

BACK
Using 2¾ mm (no. 12) needles, cast on 82 sts.
Rib 14 rows.
Change to 3 mm (no. 11) needles and stocking st 52 rows.
Next row: cast off 5 sts, at beginning of next 2 rows.
Next row: k1, sl. 1, k1, psso, knit to last 3 sts, k2tog, k1.
Next row: purl.
Repeat these last 2 rows until 26 sts remain.
Cast off.

LEFT FRONT
Using 2¾ mm (no. 12) needles, cast on 60 sts.
Rib 14 rows, starting k1, p1, and ending k2.
Change to 3 mm (no. 11) needles.

Row 1: knit to last 6 sts, rib 6.
Row 2: rib 6, purl to end.
Repeat last 2 rows 3 times.
Next row: knit to last 8 sts, k2tog, rib 6.
Next row: rib 6, purl to end.
Next row: knit to last 8 sts, k2tog, rib 6.
Next row: rib 6, purl to end.
Next row: knit to last 6 sts, rib 6.
Next row: rib 6, purl to end.
Repeat last 6 rows until 45 sts remain, finishing with a purl row.
Next row: cast off 5 sts, knit to last 8 sts, k2tog, rib 6.
Next row: rib 6, purl to end.
Now, keeping continuity of front decreases correct, dec 1 st at armhole edge (k1, sl.1, psso), on next and every alt. row until 14 sts remain.

Continue to decrease at armhole edge only until 6 sts remain.
Rib 22 rows, on these 6 sts.
Cast off in rib.

RIGHT FRONT
Using 2¾ mm (no. 12) needles, cast on 60 sts and work 4 rows in rib, beginning k1, p1.
Next row: rib 3, yfwd, k2tog, rib 28, yfwd, k2tog, rib to end.
Rib 9 more rows.
Change to 3 mm (no. 11) needles.
Row 1: rib 6, knit to end.
Row 2: purl to last 6 sts, rib 6.
Row 3: rib 3, yfwd, k2tog, p1, k27, yfwd, k2tog, knit to end.
Row 4: purl to last 6 sts, rib 6.
Row 5: rib 6, knit to end.
Row 6: purl to last 6 sts, rib 6.
Row 7: as row 5.

Row 8: as row 6.
Row 9: rib 6, k1, sl.1, k1, psso, knit to end.
Row 10: purl to last 6 sts, rib 6.
Row 11: as row 9.
Row 12: as row 10.
Row 13: rib 6, knit to end.
Row 14: as row 10.
Repeat rows 9 to 14 until 44 sts remain.
Cast off 5 sts, purl to last 6 sts, rib 6.
Keeping continuity of front decreases correct, dec. 1 st at armhole edge (work to last 3 sts, k2tog, k1) on next and every alt. row until 14 sts remain.
Continue to decrease at armhole edge only until 6 sts remain.
Rib 22 rows on these 6 sts.
Cast off in rib.

SLEEVES

Using 2¾ mm (no. 12) needles, cast on 36 sts.
Work 10 rows in rib.
Change to 3 mm (no. 11) needles.
Next row: knit.
Next row: purl.
Inc. 1 st at each end of next and every 4th row until 58 sts.
Stocking st 17 rows without increasing.
Cast off 5 sts at beginning of next 2 rows.
Row 1: k1, sl.1, k1, psso, knit to last 3 sts, k2tog, k1.
Row 2: k1, purl to last st, k1.
Row 3: knit.
Row 4: k1, purl to last st, k1.
Repeat last 4 rows once, then 1st and 2nd rows only until 6 sts.
Cast off.

TO MAKE UP

Join the side seams of the body. Stitch the sleeve seams together and sew the sleeve into position. Join the ends of the neckband and stitch round the back of the neck. Attach the buttons to correspond with buttonholes. Use 3 strands of embroidery silk to sew 2 french knots in the middle of the buttons.

Using 3 strands of embroidery silk, work embroidery (see page 85) running up the inside of rib border as shown in the photograph. The rosebuds are worked in pale apricot with apricot centres and pale green leaves, followed by 2 french knots in apricot. Work a rosebud with leaves on each cuff.

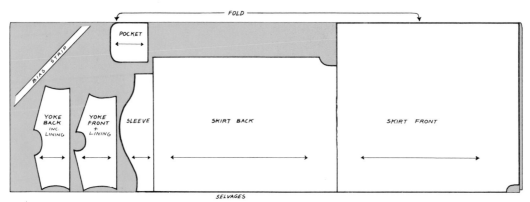

Cutting layout for dress 90 cm (36 in)

115 cm (45 in)

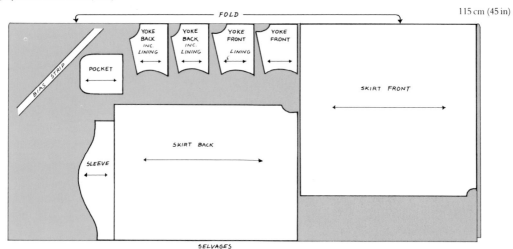

SMOCKED DRESS

Size: 18 months

MATERIALS

*1.5 metres (1²⁄₃) yards, apricot patterned
polyester cotton, cotton lawn or similar, 90 cm
(36 in) wide or 1.5 metres (1²⁄₃ yards) ×
115 cm (45 in)
50 cm (½ yard), white voile or cotton lawn,
90 cm (36 in) or 115 cm (45 in) wide
2 skeins, pale green embroidery silk
3 skeins, pale apricot embroidery silk
1 skein, apricot embroidery silk
4 small white buttons with star-shaped cut-out
1 small press-stud, size 00*

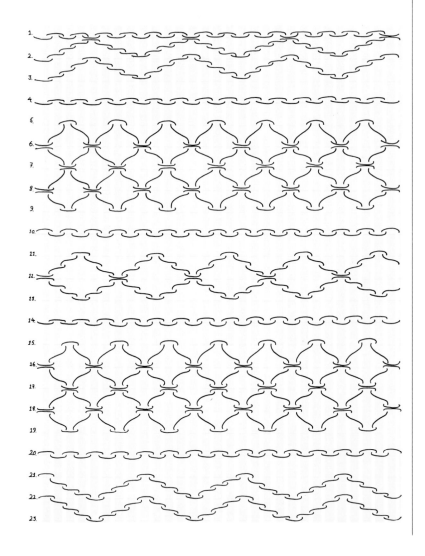

SMOCKING PATTERN F:
*work rows 1, 4 to 9, 15 to
19 in pale apricot, rest pale
green. Omit the last row on
backs.*

THE PATTERN

Enlarge the pattern pieces given on pages 92 and 93. Following the diagrams on page 83, lay and cut out the pattern from the apricot material, including one bias strip 3 × 36 cm (1¼ × 14¼ in) for the binding around the neckline and two 3 × 23 cm (1¼ × 9 in) for the sleeve edging. Mark all dots, crosses and buttonholes with tailor's tacks.

THE SMOCKING

1. Following the smocking instructions, page 116, make 23 rows of gathering on the front skirt and 22 rows on the skirt backs. Pull up the gathering until the material is slightly narrower than the corresponding yoke. Using 2 strands of embroidery silk, smock pattern F across the gathering. Smock the shortened version on the backs (omitting the last row of the smocking pattern).
2. From the white voile, cut 2 strips (NB *not* on the bias) 3 × 36 cm (1¼ × 14¼ in) and 1 strip 3 × 53 cm (1¼ × 22 in). Roll 1 edge of the strips and whip with 2 strands of apricot embroidery silk. (See techniques section, page 109.)

TO MAKE THE DRESS

3. Follow the instructions for the Smocked Dress for a 12 month old, page 66, from step 3 to step 10 inclusive.
4. Pull up the gathers on the lower edge of the sleeve until it is the same length as one of the bias strips for the sleeve – 3 × 23 cm (1¼ × 9 in). Spread the gathers evenly.
5. Join the side edges of the sleeve with a french seam.
6. Attach the gathered whipped strips for the ruffle to the sleeve edges as described in the techniques section, page 108. Finish the sleeves with bias binding.

7. Continue with the instructions for the 12 month dress, from step 15 to 21 inclusive, attaching the ruffle to the neckline before the bias strip.
8. Continue with steps 23 to 25 inclusive of the instructions for the 12 month dress, using 3 strands of embroidery silk to sew on the buttons with 2 french knots, 1 in apricot, 1 in pale green.

FINISHING THE DRESS

9. Turn in a small hem on the top of the pockets and slipstitch. Match the dots on the pockets with the dots on the skirt front. Turn under seam allowance and stitch in place.
10. Embroider the neck and sleeve bindings as illustrated in diagram below.

Cutting layout for buster suit 90 cm (36 in)

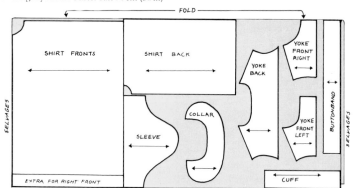

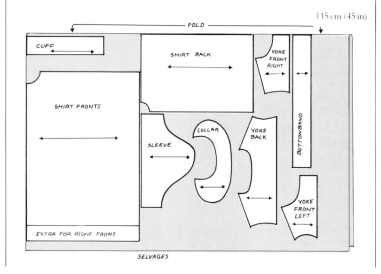

From about eighteen months buster suits are a great favourite with Nanny for her male charges. Very occasionally a romper may be seen on a tiny tot of this age at a party but the majority wear buster suits for both every-day and parties. The younger toddler will wear crawler pants buttoned on to a co-ordinating shirt; from two years he will wear straight button-on shorts. Nanny is rarely seen struggling to keep her charge tucked in, as these button-on bottoms prevent shirt and vest from escaping, with the result that the toddler remains tidy whilst playing, without being constantly fussed over. Nanny will also make sure that the trouser legs are of a suitable length, not so short that the nappy or pants can be seen, nor so long as the more modern bermudas.

The buster suit pattern I have given has a smocked shirt which will fit with either the button-on crawler pants or the straight shorts. The shirt may be white with contrasting bottoms, as in the photograph on page 89, or both parts may be made from the same coloured material. With the crawler pants the back waistband fastens on to the side buttons first, followed by the front.

BUSTER SUIT
Size: 18 months
MATERIALS
1.1 metres (1¼ yards), white Viyella, Clydella or similar, 90 cm (36 in) wide or 90 cm (36 in) × 115 cm (45 in)
50 cm (½ yard), navy Viyella, Clydella or similar, 90 cm (36 in) or 115 cm (45 in) wide
2 skeins, navy embroidery silk
scrap of red embroidery silk
6 small white buttons with 4 holes
6 medium white buttons with 4 holes
50 cm (½ yard), narrow elastic, 6 mm (¼ in) wide

THE PATTERN
Enlarge the pattern pieces given on pages 94 to 99 for the shirt and bottoms.
Following the diagrams on page 85 for the shirt and page 90 for the bottoms, lay and cut out the pattern, cutting the shirt from the white material and the bottoms from the navy. Mark all dots, crosses and buttonholes with tailor's tacks.

THE SMOCKING

RIGHT SHIRT FRONT

1. Turn under 3 cm (1¼ in) along the buttonband edge and press. Beginning 4.5 cm (1¾ in) from the buttonband edge, fold a 1.5 cm (⅝ in) pleat along the lines from the dots at the top of the piece to the dots at the hem edge. Pin in place at the top and bottom only. Press the pleats in, for 20 cm (8 in) from the bottom. It is easier to do 2 at a time.

LEFT SHIRT FRONT

2. Turn *up* 1.5 cm (⅝ in) along the buttonband edge and press. Beginning 4.5 cm (1¾ in) from the edge, fold a 1.5 cm (⅝ in) pleat along the lines from the dots at the top to the dots at the hem edge. Pin in place at top and bottom edge only. Press the pleats in, for 20 cm (8 in) from the bottom.

BOTH FRONTS

3. Remove the pins from the pleats. Leaving 2.5 cm (1 in) free from the buttonband, make 13 rows of gathering for the smocking, following the instructions in the techniques section, page 116. Pull up the gathering until it is spread evenly to a width of 12 cm (4¾ in), leaving 1 cm (⅜ in) ungathered at the armhole edge for the seam. Refold the pleats into the material and pin along the hem edge only. Using 2 strands of embroidery silk, smock and embroider pattern G across the gathering.

TO MAKE THE BUSTER SUIT

JOINING THE SHIRT AND YOKES

4. Opening out the turn-up at the buttonband edge, align the left front yoke with the left shirt front, *right* sides together. Make certain that all corresponding dots and crosses are matching and that the unsmocked portion of the front is in the correct position. Pin the top edge of the shirt to the lower edge of the yoke. Spread the fullness evenly and tack in place. Stitch across the seam, then press the seam towards the yoke. Press the turn-up along the buttonband again, extending the fold all the way up to the yoke.

5. Place the *right* sides of the right front yoke and the right shirt front together, matching all corresponding dots and crosses. Spread the fullness evenly and check that the unsmocked portion of the body is in the correct position. Pin the top edge of the shirt to the lower edge of the yoke, allowing the yoke lining to extend beyond the buttonband edge. Tack in place, then stitch across the seam. Press the seam towards the yoke.

6. Remove all the guide threads from the smocking.

7. With the *right* side of the shirt back facing, fold the material along the line indicated, so that the crosses meet in the middle over the centre dot. Press, then pin at the top and hem edge. The top edge of the shirt back should now be the same width as the back yoke.

8. Align the top edge of the shirt back against the yoke back and pin in place. Tack, then stitch across the seam. Press the seam towards the yoke.

9. Join the front and back yokes at the shoulder with a plain seam.

Leave the lining of the right front yoke hanging free. Press the seams open.

10. Using a french seam join the side seams of the shirt fronts and back. Press.

THE SLEEVES

11. With the *right* side of the cuff against the *wrong* side of the sleeve, pin the cuff edge to the lower edge of the sleeve. Stitch across. Trim the seam allowance and press upwards. At the same time press in the 1 cm (⅜ in) seam allowance along the other edge of the cuff.

12. Fold the cuff completely over to the right side of the sleeve and press along the seam line. Topstitch in place 3 mm (⅛ in) in from the top edge of the cuff.

13. Join the side edges of the cuff/sleeve with a french seam.

14. Turn the shirt inside out and, with *right* sides together, align the side seams of the sleeve with the side seams of the shirt. Pin in place. Align the centre dot of the sleeve with the shoulder seam of the yoke and pin in place. Beginning at the sleeve seam again, continue to pin up both edges of the armhole until the centre top has almost been reached. At both sides of the centre dot fold the excess material over on the inside of the sleeve towards the centre (making a box pleat on the right side) and pin in place. Tack around the armhole, then stitch the seam. Press the seam away from the sleeve.

15. Neaten the lower edges of the armhole seams, between the front and back yokes, with machine whipping, or by hand with blanket stitch.

THE BUTTONBAND

16. With the *right* side of the buttonband against the *wrong* side of the left shirt front and beginning 1 cm (⅜ in) down from

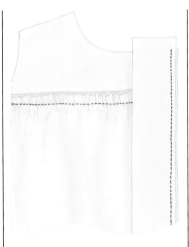

the top edge of the buttonband, align the side edges and pin along the fold line, as shown in the diagram. Stitch down this line.

17. Trim the seam allowance and press. At the same time press inwards the 1 cm (⅜ in) seam allowance along the other edge of the buttonband.

18. Fold the buttonband completely over to the *right* side of the shirt and press along the seam line. Topstitch in place 3 mm (⅛ in) in from this edge and also 3 mm (⅛ in) from the folded edge of the buttonband.

19. Trim the top edge of the buttonband to the shape of the yoke neckline.

THE COLLAR

20. With *right* sides together, pin the under collar to the upper collar around the outside edge. NB The seam allowance here is only 6 mm (¼ in). Tack and stitch around this edge.

21. Trim the seam allowance and turn the collar *right* side out. Press the edge.

22. Pin the collar and shirt together, *right* sides up, around the neckline. Tack, then stitch in place. Trim and clip the seam.

THE LINING

23. Join the front and back yoke

Smocked buster suit with button-on pants (see page 86) for an 18 month old boy and a version with short trousers (page 91) for a 2 year old.

linings at the shoulders, *right* sides together, with a plain seam, not forgetting the left yoke lining. Press the seams open.

24. Fold the lining over and with the *wrong* sides together, pin the yoke lining to the yoke and collar around the neckline, aligning the corresponding shoulder seams.

25. On the inside, turn under the seam allowances on the front and back yoke linings. Press the yoke/sleeve seams inwards and pin the lining over this and the yoke/shirt seams. Slipstitch in place (thus enclosing all raw edges.) Turn under the right front lining side edge and slipstitch to the back of the buttonband.

THE NECKLINE

26. Take the pins out of the neckline and turn the seam allowance into the lining along the stitch line. Turn in the seam allowance of the lining and slipstitch to the stitch line of the collar. Extend the turn-in along the buttonbands and neatly slipstitch on the inside of the shirt.

FINISHING THE SHIRT

27. Take out the pins that are holding the pleats in place. Make a narrow 6 mm (¼ in) hem along the bottom edge of the shirt. Fold the pleats back, including the back pleats and overstitch in place along the hem only.

28. Make buttonholes in the positions shown on the pattern. Using 3 strands of embroidery silk, sew the small buttons in corresponding places, with 2 straight stitches. Sew 2 of the medium buttons on the side seam lines in the position indicated on the pattern, and the other 4 medium buttons on the shirt body where indicated, again with 2 straight stitches and using embroidery silk.

29. Using 2 strands of embroidery silk, overstitch down

both edges of the buttonband, round the collar, round the top edges of the cuffs, and across the back yoke. An overstitch every 2 machine stitches is a rough guide as to how big they should be.

THE BOTTOMS – FRONTS AND BACK

30. Neaten the side edges of the front for 7.5 cm (3 in) from the top edge down to the cross marked on the pattern, with a very tiny 3 mm (⅛ in) hem.

31. Neaten the side edges of the back for 9 cm (3½ in) from the top edge down to the cross marked on the pattern, in the same manner as the front.

32. Join the side edges of the front and back with a french seam, from the casing edge to 6 mm (¼ in) over the neatened side edges. This leaves an opening from the top edge of the front 7 cm (2¾ in) long and in the back 8.5 cm (3¼ in) long.

THE WAISTBAND

33. Make 2 rows of machine gathering stitches between the crosses on the top edges of the front and back.

34. Taking the front, pull up the gathers until the front is the same length as the waistband. Leave the centre 7.5 cm (3 in) sparsely gathered. Repeat with the back but spreading the fullness evenly across.

35. Place the *right* side of the front against the *right* side of one edge

of the waistband, matching centre dots. Pin, then stitch across the seam. Trim the seam allowances.

36. Fold the waistband over in half. Turn in the seam allowance at both ends (this will also turn in side openings) and pin. On the inside turn under the remaining seam allowance (removing side pins when necessary) and pin to seam line. Slipstitch in place. The waistband should now be 3 cm (1¼ in) wide. Repeat for back waistband.

37. Remove any gathering stitches that show.

38. Topstitch along the folded edge.

THE LEG CASINGS

39. Join the centre 8 cm (3¼ in) of the back and front at the casing edges between the dots marked on the pattern, with a 13 mm (½ in) wide plain seam.

40. Make a narrow 1 cm (⅜ in) casing round the bottom edge on both sides of the centre seam.

41. Thread 23 cm (9 in) of elastic (adjust here if necessary to width of baby's leg) through both leg casings and secure at each end with several stitches on the inside.

42. Returning to the centre seam turn under the raw edges and carefully slipstitch in place. (These stitches should show as little as possible on the right side.)

43. Work the buttonholes on the waistband in the positions shown, 2 in the centre of front and back and 2 at the sides.

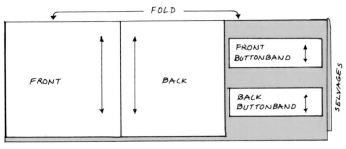

90 & 115 cm (36 & 45 in)

SMOCKING PATTERN G: *in navy with red bullion knots.*

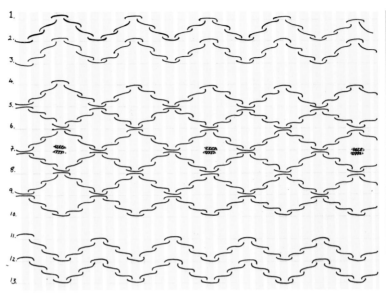

SHORT TROUSERS

SIZE: 2 YEARS

MATERIALS

50 cm (½ yard) red corduroy, needlecord or similar, 90 cm (36 in) or 115 cm (45 in) wide
1 metre (1 yard) red seam binding, 13 mm (½ in) wide
8 medium buttons (to sew on to the shirt)

The 18 month size shirt will fit with these shorts to make a Buster Suit for a 2 year old and still leave room for growth. Alter the position of the buttons on the shirt to correspond with the buttonholes on the shorts.

THE PATTERN

Enlarge the pattern pieces given on page 98. Following the diagram below right, lay and cut out the pattern. Take care that the tops of both pieces are in the same direction if using corduroy or any material with a nap. Mark all dots and buttonholes with tailor's tacks.

TO MAKE THE SHORTS

1. Prepare each piece of the pattern by machine whipping, or by hand by blanket stitch, down the side, centre and leg seams.
2. With *right* sides together, stitch down the centre of the front, then the back with a plain seam. Clip the curves a little, and press the seam open.
3. Join the front to the back, *right* sides together, by stitching a plain seam down the side edges. Open out the seams and press.
4. Using a plain seam, join the inner legs, again pressing the seam open.
5. Turn in 1 cm (⅜ in) along the upper edge of the shorts, then fold another 3 cm (1¼ in) over to the inside. Tack in place, then stitch close to the edge by machine.
6. On the *right* side, topstitch along the fold at the upper edge of the shorts.
7. Pin the seambinding on the *right* side of the leg hemline and

stitch. Press up the hem allowance to the inside and slipstitch the binding in place. A normal hem can be worked here, but does look rather bulky if using thick cord material.
8. Work the buttonholes in the positions marked.

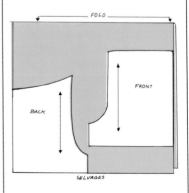

90 & 115 cm (36 & 45 in)

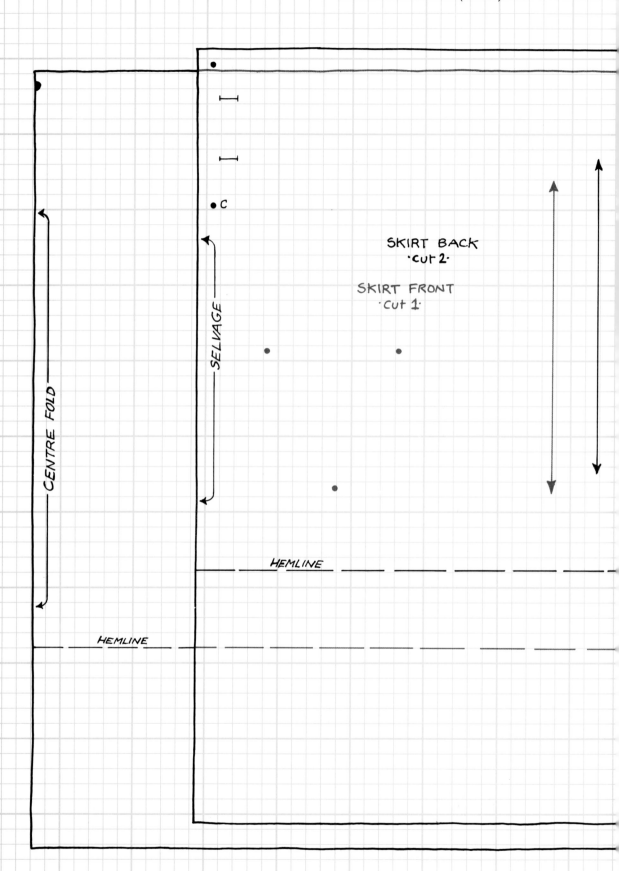

SKIRT BACK
·cut 2·

SKIRT FRONT
·cut 1·

SELVAGE

CENTRE FOLD

• C

HEMLINE

HEMLINE

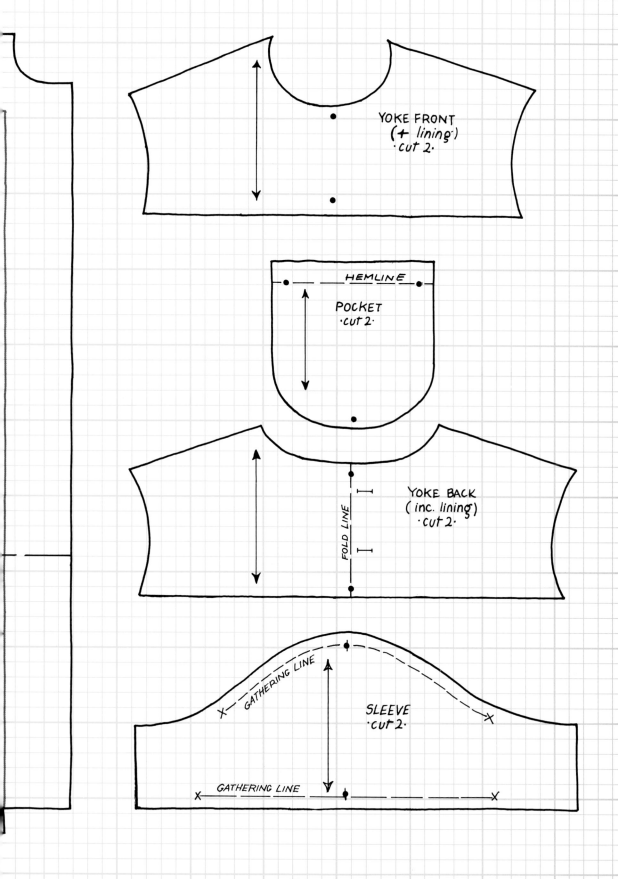

YOKE FRONT
(+ lining)
·cut 2·

HEMLINE

POCKET
·cut 2·

YOKE BACK
(inc. lining)
·cut 2·

FOLD LINE

GATHERING LINE

SLEEVE
·cut 2·

GATHERING LINE

BUSTER SUIT SHIRT

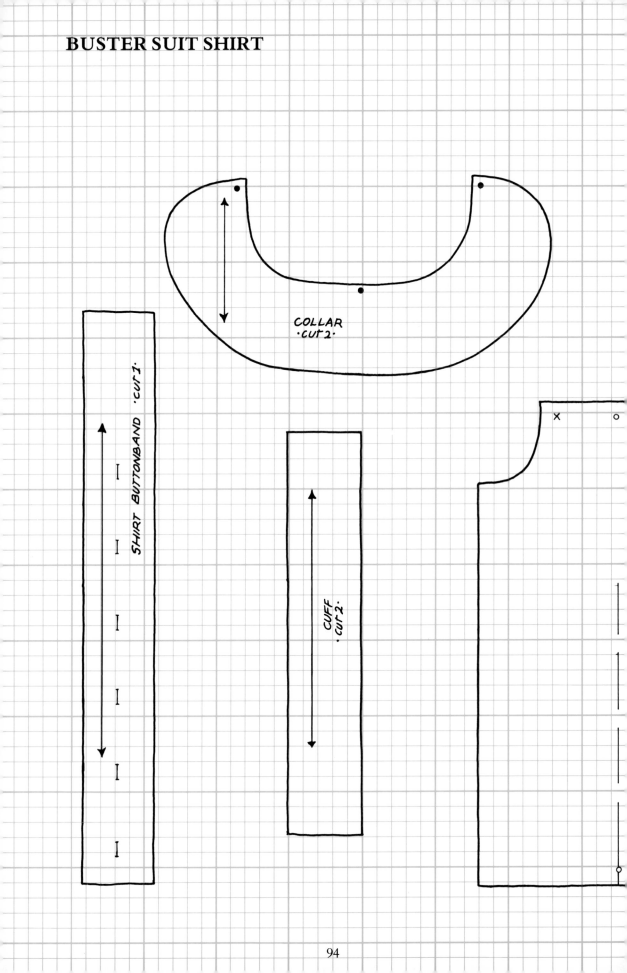

COLLAR
·CUT 2·

SHIRT BUTTONBAND ·CUT 1·

CUFF
·CUT 2·

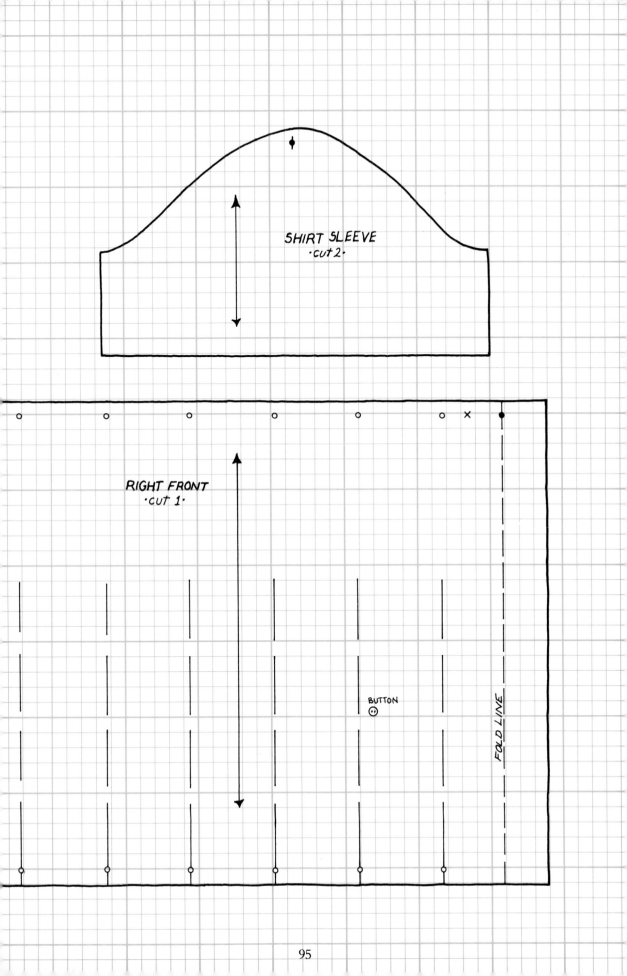

SHIRT SLEEVE
·cut 2·

RIGHT FRONT
·cut 1·

BUTTON

FOLD LINE

95

BUSTER SUIT SHIRT

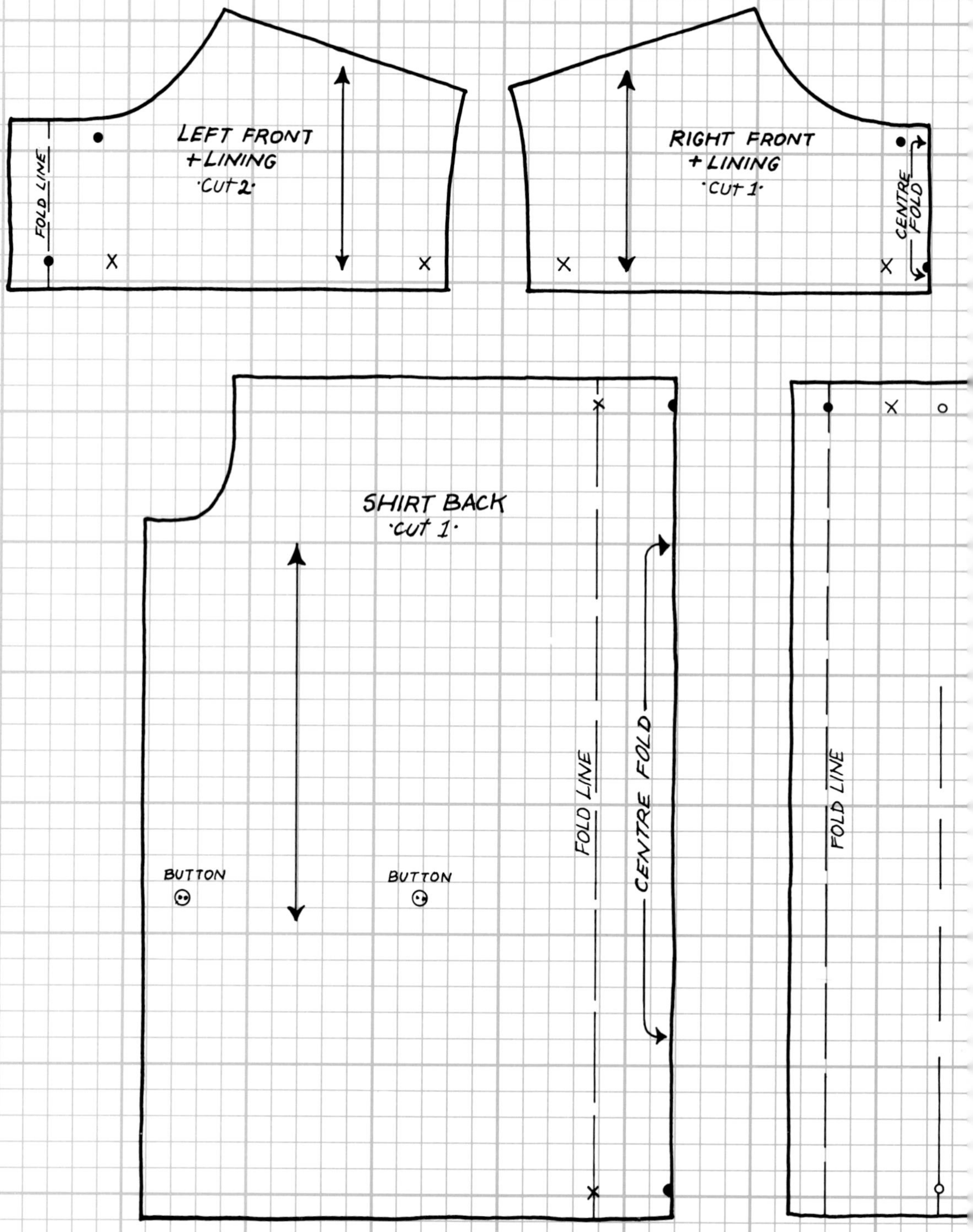

LEFT FRONT
+ LINING
·CUT 2·

FOLD LINE

RIGHT FRONT
+ LINING
·CUT 1·

CENTRE FOLD

SHIRT BACK
·CUT 1·

BUTTON

BUTTON

FOLD LINE

CENTRE FOLD

FOLD LINE

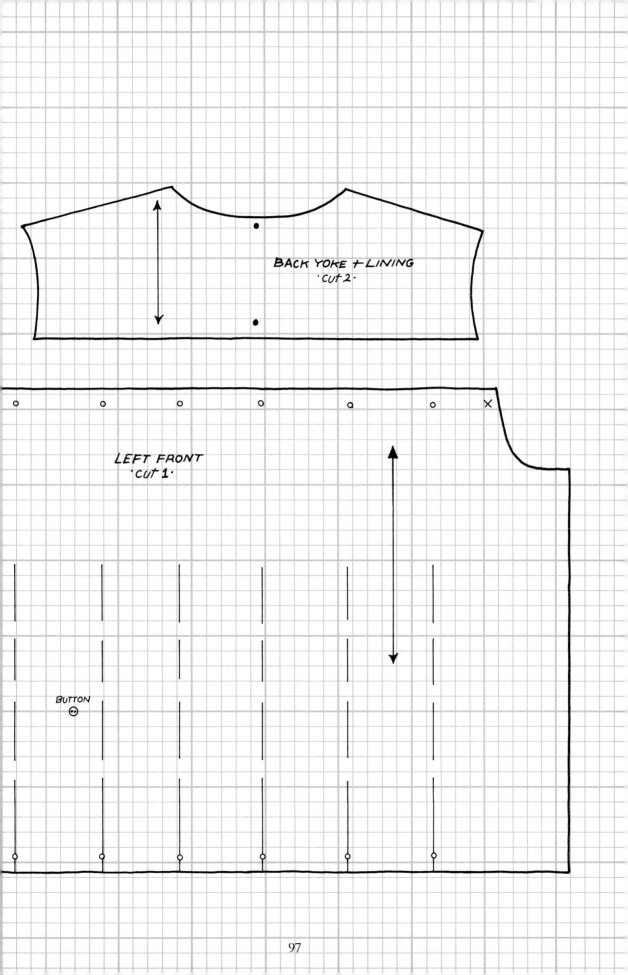

BACK YOKE + LINING
·cut 2·

LEFT FRONT
·cut 1·

BUTTON

BUSTER SUIT BOTTOMS AND SHORT TROUSERS

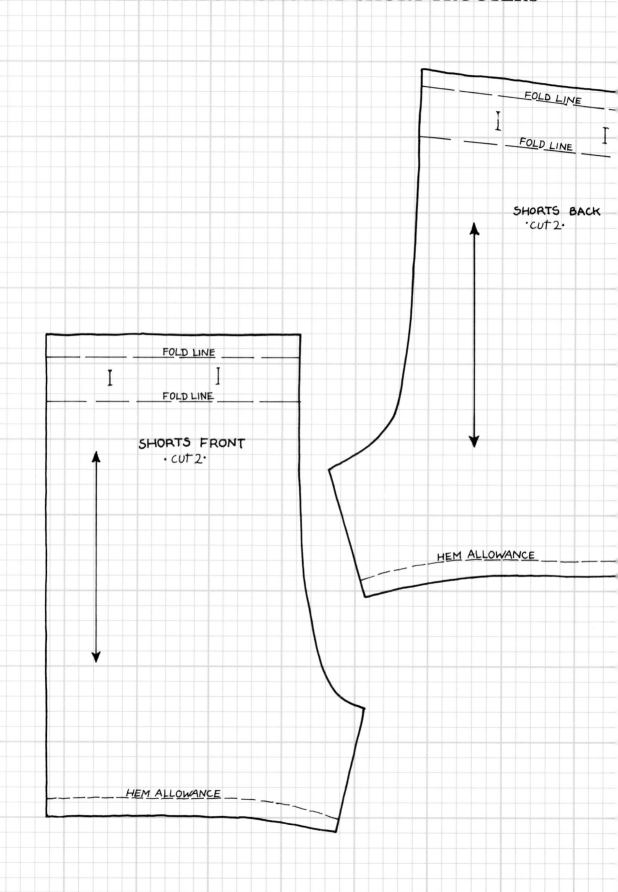

FOLD LINE

FOLD LINE

SHORTS BACK
·CUT 2·

FOLD LINE

FOLD LINE

SHORTS FRONT
·CUT 2·

HEM ALLOWANCE

HEM ALLOWANCE

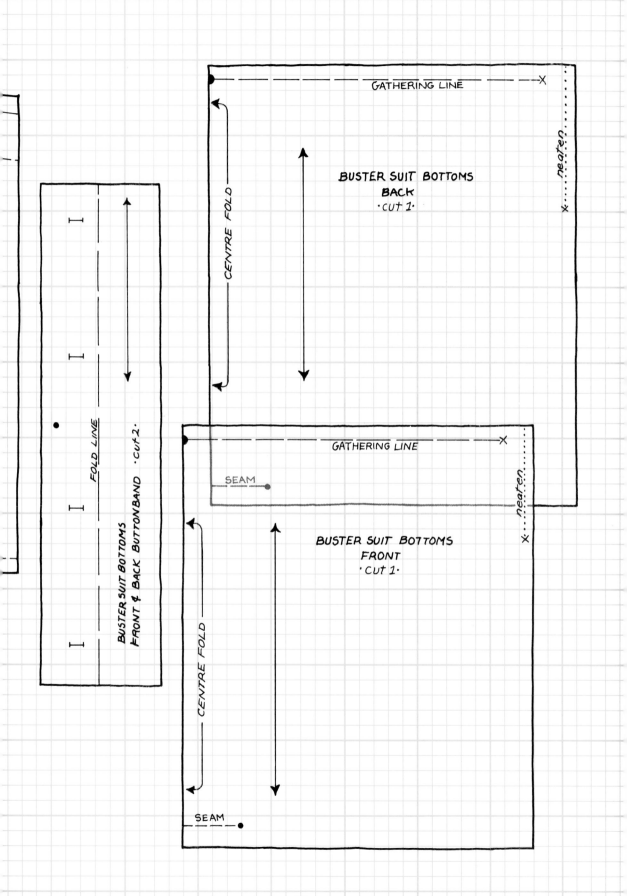

GATHERING LINE

neaten

BUSTER SUIT BOTTOMS
BACK
·CUT 1·

CENTRE FOLD

FOLD LINE

BUSTER SUIT BOTTOMS
FRONT & BACK BUTTONBAND ·CUT 2·

GATHERING LINE

neaten

SEAM

BUSTER SUIT BOTTOMS
FRONT
·CUT 1·

CENTRE FOLD

SEAM

BASIC TECHNIQUES

KNITTING

CASTING ON

There are three methods of casting on but only two of them are used in this book. Unless the pattern specifically says otherwise the first method should be used. This gives a purled edge which is neater but the two needle method leaves the stitches looser and therefore is chosen where the cast-on stitches are to be knitted into the garment.

1. Start by making a slip knot roughly 60 cm (24 in) from the beginning of the wool.

★ Place the needle upwards through the loop. Hold this needle in your right hand and, using the loose length of wool, make a loop in an anti-clockwise direction around your left thumb. Now place the needle upwards through the loop on your thumb and pass the wool from the ball under and over the needle. Bring the point of the needle through the loop, carrying the wool with it, so making another loop.

Pull up and leave this loop on the needle.

Repeat from ★ until the required number of stitches has been made.

2. TWO NEEDLE METHOD

Starting a short distance from the beginning of the wool, make a loose slip knot around one needle. Hold this needle in your left hand.

★ Place the other needle upwards through the loop behind the first needle. Now pass the wool from the ball behind the two needles and up and over the second needle. Bring the point of the right hand needle, carrying with it the wool, through the loop on the left hand needle. The loop just made should then be put on to the left hand needle.

Repeat from ★ until the required number of stitches has been made.

CASTING OFF

Work two stitches according to the pattern (knit, purl, rib or moss st). With the left hand needle, lift the first stitch over the second one, allowing it to drop under the right hand needle. This casts off one stitch.

Repeat until the required number of stitches has been cast off, see diagram page 102. If finishing off a whole row, continue in this way until one loop is left. Remove this from the needle, break off the wool and pass it through the loop, pulling it tight. The end of the wool is darned into the garment seam.

STITCHES

RIB STITCH

This stitch is used where a small amount of stretching is needed. When casting on, the number of stitches must be divisible by two.

★ Knit 1 stitch, purl 1 stitch and repeat from ★ to the end of the row. Work each row like this until the desired number has been reached.

Rib stitch should always begin k1, p1, unless otherwise specified. Occasionally in this book ribbing begins with k2,

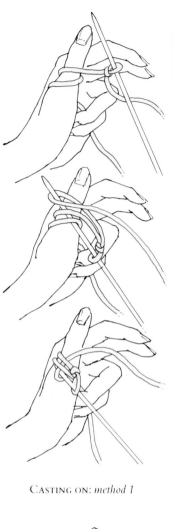

CASTING ON: *method 1*

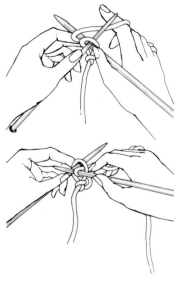

CASTING ON: *2 needle method*

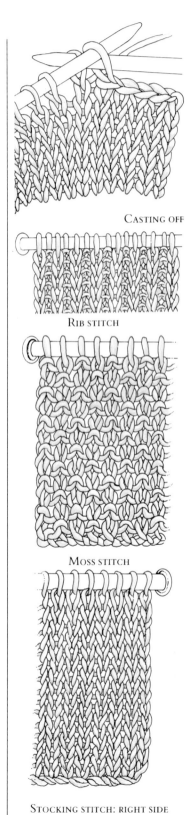

CASTING OFF

RIB STITCH

MOSS STITCH

STOCKING STITCH: RIGHT SIDE

as this gives a neater finish for buttonbands, but it is always mentioned within the text of the pattern if this is necessary.

MOSS STITCH

With moss stitch an odd number of stitches is needed. ★ Knit 1 stitch, purl 1 stitch and repeat from ★ to the end of the first row. On the return row, repeat the knit 1, purl 1. The odd number of stitches means you are knitting every stitch knitted in the first row and purling each purled stitch, which is just the opposite of ribbing.

STOCKING STITCH

This stitch is made by knitting one row and purling the next. On two needles this stitch is made by continuing to alternate knit and purl rows until the desired length is reached. It is always begun with a knit row.

SLIPPING STITCHES

To slip a stitch, insert the right needle into the stitch and slide off the left needle without working, taking care not to twist stitches.

INCREASING

When it is necessary to add to the number of stitches, work as follows: Knit or purl into the stitch in the normal way but before slipping it off the needle, knit or purl into the back of the stitch a second time. Slip both loops on to the right needle.

DECREASING

There are two methods which can be used:

1. Knit or purl two stitches together.
2. Slip a stitch, without working, on to the right needle. Work the next stitch, then pass the slipped one over the one just worked, letting it drop off the needle.

JOINING WOOL

When wool from another ball is needed in the middle of a piece it is always better to join it at the beginning of a row. Leave the end of the wool on the previous row and begin knitting the following row with the new wool. The loose ends can be darned into the garment on the wrong side afterwards.

CROCHET CHAIN CORD

Begin by making a slip knot around the crochet hook. Place the hook under the thread from left to right and draw through the loop already on the hook. Repeat this action until the cord is the necessary length, then cut the thread and pull the last loop completely through. Sew the loose ends back down the cord a little way.

CROCHET CHAIN STITCH ON KNITTING

Taking the knitted article, right side facing, in the left hand and the crochet hook in the right, place the hook through the desired stitch on the cast-on edge of the knitting. Catch the contrasting thread and pull through the cast-on stitch, leaving the loop on the crochet hook. Place the hook through the next cast-on stitch, catch the contrasting thread and pull through both the cast-on stitch and the loop already on the hook. This leaves one loop only on the hook.

Repeat until the desired length is completed. Pull the last loop completely through and cut off. Darn the loose ends into the garment on the wrong side.

This stitch can also be made along a border edge of a garment.

JOINING TWO PIECES OF KNITTING

Place the edges to be joined right sides together and pin. Using the same ply wool as the article knitted, or the loose ends from the cast-on or cast-off edge, overstitch (see page 106) along the seam. Darn any loose ends of wool into the garment, preferably into the seams. It is best to cut any sewn-in wool 13 mm (½ in) away from the knitting. This allows the knitting to stretch without the darned wool becoming unravelled.

BUTTONHOLES AND BUTTONS

The instructions for buttonholes are usually given within the patterns but can be made in the following manner: k1, p1, yfwd, k2tog, then continue in pattern to the end of the row.

The easiest way to judge where to sew on the buttons is to lay the buttonhole-band over the buttonband and, through each buttonhole, catch a stitch of the buttonband with a dressmaker's pin. Leaving the pins in position, carefully ease the pins through the buttonholes, so that the buttonhole-band can be lifted off, leaving the pins in the buttonband in the correct positions.

Buttons with a star-shaped cut-out are sewn on with french knots as in the embroidery instructions, see page 111.

SEWING

TO MAKE THE PATTERNS

The patterns in this book are all drawn to scale on a squared background and each square represents 1 cm (⅜ in). This makes for easy enlarging of the patterns as dressmakers' paper already squared off to this size can be bought. A more laborious method is to draw 1 cm (⅜ in) squares on to large pieces of blank paper.

Copy the pattern on to the squared paper using a pencil, so that mistakes can be rubbed out. To make straight lines, horizontally or vertically, count up the squares and mark the beginning and end of the line with a dot on the paper. Using a ruler to keep the line straight, connect the dots. For straight lines running at an angle, make a mark on your paper at each point where the pattern lines cross the squared grid, then join the marks using a ruler.

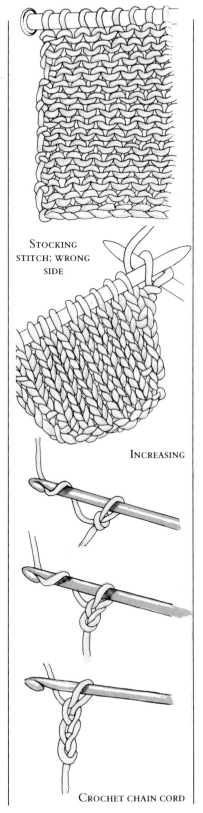

STOCKING STITCH: WRONG SIDE

INCREASING

CROCHET CHAIN CORD

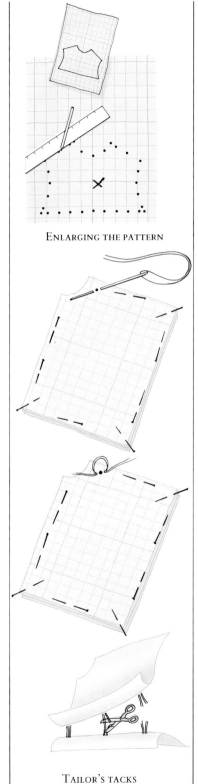

ENLARGING THE PATTERN

TAILOR'S TACKS

Curved lines are made in a similar manner, marking each point on your paper in the position where the pattern lines cross the squared grid, then carefully joining the marks freehand, copying the curves shown on the pattern. Lightly sketch them in at first, then mark with a definite line, when they are in the correct position.

Copy all the other pattern markings, such as the centre dots, buttonholes, gathering lines, in the correct positions and label each piece. Cut the enlarged patterns out.

LAY OUT

Once the material is cut, mistakes cannot be rectified, so take great care in laying and cutting out the pattern. Unless otherwise stated, 1 cm (3/8 in) has been allowed for seams.

First collect together all the pieces needed for the garment chosen and identify which have to be placed on a fold or selvage and whether any pieces are used again. (Some patterns have linings incorporated, some need a pattern piece to be cut twice and some have separate lining pieces.)

Fold the material according to the cutting layout diagram – usually in half lengthways. Lay the pattern pieces on the material in the positions shown. All pattern pieces are marked with an arrow. Match this to the weave of the material when laying the pieces.

Corduroy, velvet, satin and materials with a one-way design have a 'nap' and it is important to lay the pattern pieces with their tops pointing in the same direction. Ensure that the pieces with edges which need to be on a fold or selvage are so placed.

Pin the pieces to the material using plenty of pins, especially on curves and long straight lines. Cut exactly along the edges of the pattern, using sharp scissors with long blades and finishing one piece completely before beginning the next.

Mark all dots, crosses and buttonholes with tailor's tacks (see below) before removing the paper pattern. Although it may seem tedious, it is worth spending the time to do this, as I have only used the minimum of markings, where they really are necessary.

CUTTING BIAS STRIPS

A true bias strip is made when the material is cut at a 45° angle across the weave. A bias strip, however, can be cut at a lesser degree than this, so long as it runs in a direction away from the straight weave of the material.

STITCHES

TAILOR'S TACKS

This is a quick way of transferring markings from the paper pattern piece to the material.

Take one piece at a time whilst it is still pinned to the paper pattern.

Thread the needle with a long piece of cotton in a contrasting colour to the material and double it but do not make a knot.

At the point to be marked, insert the needle from the top and make a small stitch through all the layers. Pull the thread until only the last 4 cm (1½ in) remain on the surface. Make a small back stitch in the same spot and pull the thread until a loop is formed, roughly the same length as the end thread. Cut the thread 4 cm (1½ in) away from the pattern. When all necessary tacks have been made, remove the pins and gently pull the paper pattern away from the material as far as the loop will stretch, without pulling out the tack. Holding on to the tack, remove the paper pattern, tearing a small hole where the tack is made. If this is done carefully, the pattern can still be used again. If there are two layers of material, cut the stitches apart between them. Cotton threads will remain on both pieces of material.

TACKING

This is a temporary line stitched by machine, or with a small running stitch (see below) by hand, through both layers of material, parallel with the edges. It is wise for beginners to tack every seam before sewing but, with only a little experience, it is possible to tack only in the places instructed and still achieve a good result.

SLIPSTITCH

Slipstitches are used when the stitches need to be seen as little as possible, mostly when making a hem or when sewing down a folded edge.

Work with the folded edge towards you and from the right to left. Make a knot and insert the needle into fold, bringing it through to the side facing you. (The knot is now hidden under the fold.) Pick up a tiny amount of the material just under the fold with the needle and pull the thread through. Reinsert the needle into the fold, slipping it along the inside for about 2.5 cm (1 in) on hems and 1 cm (⅜ in) on all other work. Bring the needle and thread out through the fold and carry on in this manner, stitching into the material and fold by turns.

TOPSTITCH

Topstitching is literally what it says, stitching on the top of the material. The stitching is usually sewn on top of a fold and as close to the edge as possible. It is preferably stitched by a machine but may be done by hand with very tiny running stitches. Topstitching does much towards giving a garment a professional finish.

If two rows of topstitching are worked on the same piece of material, it is best to work the stitching from the same end each time, since if they are stitched back and forth this may cause rucks to form.

BIAS STRIPS

SLIPSTITCH

TOPSTITCHING

FLAT OR PLAIN SEAM

FRENCH SEAM

OVERCASTING

OPEN BUTTONHOLE STITCH

RUNNING STITCH

This is a hand stitch made by picking up small amounts of material with the needle in a line and pulling the thread through.

SEAMS

Seams are best stitched by machine but if a machine is not available, they may be sewn by hand using small running stitches. Unless otherwise stated a 1 cm (³⁄₈ in) seam allowance has been made in all patterns.

FLAT OR PLAIN SEAM

With right sides together, pin the material. Make a row of machine stitches 1 cm (³⁄₈ in) in from the edges. Open out the seam and press flat. All plain/flat seams require neatening with overcasting, open buttonhole stitch or machine whipping (see below), unless made on the selvage.

FRENCH SEAM

With wrong sides together, pin the material. Machine stitch 5 mm (³⁄₁₆ in) in from the edges. Trim the seam to roughly 3 mm (¹⁄₈ in) and turn the material to the wrong side. With the right sides together, pin and tack down the seam 5 mm (³⁄₁₆ in) in from the folded edge, thus enclosing the raw edges. Press the seam. Machine stitch down the seam just outside the tacking line. Remove the tacking. (If the tacking is done neatly, with small stitches, I often leave it in to give the seam extra strength.)

OVERCASTING AND MACHINE WHIPPING

These stitches are used to neaten the raw edges of a seam; overcasting by hand or on a machine, by whipping.

To overcast, make a knot in the thread and bring the needle and thread through to the front of the work. Take the needle round to the back of the material and insert it just inside the seam edge, 1 cm (³⁄₈ in) away from the previous stitch, bringing it through to the front again.

Repeat as often as necessary down the seam.

To machine whip a seam, set the machine to a medium overcast stitch according to the instructions in your manual and stitch along the edge of the seam.

OPEN BUTTONHOLE STITCH

This stitch is also used to neaten the raw edges of a seam by hand and is better at controlling the fraying of the material than overcasting.

Make a knot in the thread and, working from left to right, bring the needle and thread through to the front of the work. Insert the needle just above the material edge, pointing it downwards and letting the thread fall in a loop under the end. Pull both the needle and thread through the loop.

Repeat the stitch to the right at 6 mm (¹⁄₄ in) intervals until all the seam is edged.

CLIPPING AND TRIMMING

Curved seams often need to be clipped to help them to lie flat, whilst others may need clipping to enable the edges to spread.

To clip the seam allowance, make small cuts from the raw edge almost to the seam line, taking care not to catch the stitching.

A seam may need to be made narrower by cutting extra material away, for example in a french seam, and this is known as trimming.

To trim, cut the material along the seam line at the required distance from the stitching.

GATHERING

1. Consult the instruction manual for your sewing machine for details on how to gather material by loosening the tension.

If there are no instructions, set the stitch length to the longest setting (this is approximately 14 sts per 2.5 cm/1 in).

2. Next, with right side upwards, along the edge which is to be gathered, make two rows of stitching on either side of the seam line. (This line is 1 cm (⅜ in) from the edge.) The first row of stitching should be 6 mm (¼ in) from the edge and the second row should be 14 mm (⅝ in) from the edge.

3. Beginning at one side, take the upper two threads and draw up, spreading the gathers evenly and towards the centre. When this half is the required size, take the upper two threads from the opposite side

and again draw up, spreading the gathers evenly towards the centre as before.

For material which is to be gathered then joined and stitched to a straight pattern piece:

Follow steps 1 and 2 above, then, with right sides and edges together, pin the centre of the material with one upright pin to the centre of the straight piece. Gather as in step 3, until the width of the gathered material matches the straight piece.

4. When the gathers are evenly pinned in place all along the edge, stitch in place between the gathering threads with the gathered side upwards.

5. Withdraw any gathering threads that show on the right side of the work.

To gather by hand, make two rows of tiny running stitches in the same positions as for the machine stitching and proceed as above.

BIAS BINDING

Cut a bias strip 2 cm (¾ in) longer than the length which is to be bound and 2.5 cm (1 in) wide. (Cutting instructions are on page 104.)

JOINING BIAS STRIPS

With right sides together, place the edges to be joined, so that they overlap as in the illustration. NB The edges do not match. Pin in place. Stitch across with a plain seam 3 mm (⅛ in) from the edge. Press the tiny seam open. Cut off the bits of the seam allowance which stick out.

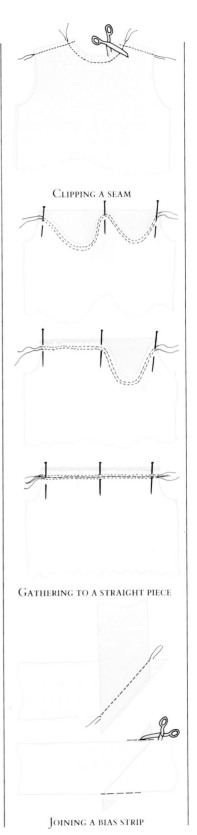

CLIPPING A SEAM

GATHERING TO A STRAIGHT PIECE

JOINING A BIAS STRIP

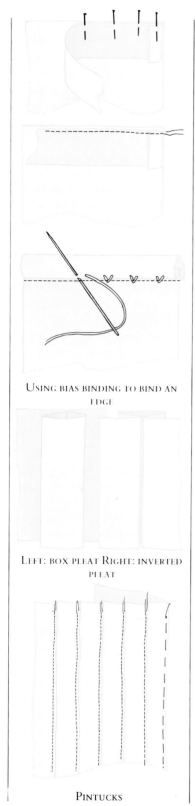

USING BIAS BINDING TO BIND AN EDGE

LEFT: BOX PLEAT RIGHT: INVERTED PLEAT

PINTUCKS

BINDING EDGES

If the edge is to have a ruffle (see page 109), gather this and place the wrong side of the ruffle against the right side of the garment, matching edges. Tack in place.

Pin one edge of the 3 cm (1¼ in) bias strip to the garment edge, right sides together, turning in 1 cm (⅜ in) at each end. Stitch 1 cm (⅜ in)\from the bias edge, i.e. along the seam line on the garment. Trim 5 mm (³⁄₁₆ in) of the seam allowances away. Fold the binding over to the wrong side, covering the raw edges as you do so.

Turn under the remaining 5 mm (³⁄₁₆ in) seam allowance on the bias strip and pin the fold to the stitching. Slipstitch in place.

This should make a 5 mm (³⁄₁₆ in) binding. Wider bindings are made in the same manner but bindings should be kept as narrow as possible, since a wide bias binding on a garment will really make it look home-made.

PLEATS, TUCKS AND PINTUCKS

A box pleat is made up of a pair of pleats placed so that they just touch, each one facing outwards away from the other.

An inverted pleat is the opposite, a pair of touching pleats which face inwards towards each other.

Tucks vary in size, when very narrow they are known as pintucks. Pintucks are traditionally used for ornamentation but tucks have the additional practical advantage of allowing extra material into a garment. These may be let down at a later stage to make room for growth.

Decide where the line for the first tuck is and fold, with wrong sides together, along this line. Stitching from the side that will be seen, topstitch (see page 105) at the desired distance from the fold: approximately 1 cm (⅜ in) from the edge for a medium tuck, 3 mm (⅛ in) from the edge for a narrow tuck and as close to the fold as possible for pintucks. Press on the wrong side, then on the right side press the tuck in the direction it is to lie.

When two or three tucks are made it is best to begin stitching from the same end, not working back and forth, as this sometimes causes rucks. When several tucks are made vertically, they may be pressed all in the same direction away from the centre, or if made down a central line (e.g. in the centre front of a yoke) they should be divided into half down the central line and pressed so that they lie in opposite directions, the right half to the right and the left half to the left.

CASINGS

Casings are used around the waist, wrist or legs, usually to contain elastic.

There are two ways of making casings:.

1. With *wrong* side up, turn in

first 3 mm (⅛ in), then 8 mm (⁵⁄₁₆ in) along the edge which is to have the casing. Pin in place. Leaving the side edges free (or a small opening) for the elastic to be inserted, machine stitch near to the inside fold. Topstitch a second row of stitching as close to the folded outer edge as possible. This second row makes a tiny heading which prevents the edge of elastic from wearing through the fold of material. This should leave sufficient room for narrow elastic 6 mm (¼ in) wide.

2. Use 13 mm (½ in) wide seam binding. Machine stitch in place along both edges of the seam binding leaving the side edges free (or a small opening) for the elastic to be inserted.

In both cases, insert the desired length of elastic through the opening. The elastic may be eased through the casing with the aid of a safety-pin on the front end of the elastic. Make a few stitches through each end of the elastic and the material to hold it in place. Sew the opening together.

HEMS

Hems are normally hand stitched with a slipstitch. A double 6– 7.5 cm (2½–3 in) hem is a good depth for a child from about 12 months old and will allow for letting down, however, skirt lengths on dresses should always be checked before sewing, as children of the same age differ so much in height.

Since materials used for children's clothes are often finer than for adults, it is necessary to fold a double hem almost down upon itself in order to prevent an unsightly line being seen through the material from the right side. Decide where the hem line is to be and turn up along this line. Turn in the raw edge until it is almost touching the inside of the outer edge fold. Pin along the inner fold. Sew the hem to the skirt with slipstitch (see page 105) or a similar hem stitch.

NARROW HEMS

Narrow hems may be made using a machine to topstitch them.

Turn in 3 mm (⅛ in) along the hem edge. Fold over another 6 mm (¼ in) and topstitch as close to the folded edge as possible.

ROLLED HEMS

Roll the raw edge of the material inwards between your finger and thumb very finely and sew a little at a time before continuing the roll. Slipstitch in place, then embroider with a close overcast stitch (see page 106), using embroidery silks of a contrasting colour.

RUFFLE

The material chosen for a ruffle should be the same weight as the main garment but it may be of contrasting colour.

Cut a strip 1½ times longer than the edge it is to trim and the desired finished width plus

CASING: 1ST METHOD

CASING: 2ND METHOD

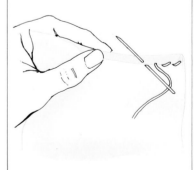

ROLLED HEM

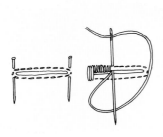

HAND-MADE BUTTONHOLE

DECORATIVE STITCHES FOR
4-HOLED BUTTONS

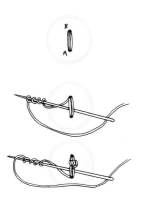

SEWING FRENCH KNOTS ON
2-HOLED BUTTONS

13 mm (½ in). Make a rolled hem along one edge, overcasting approximately every 1 cm (⅜ in) with 2 strands of embroidery silk (as explained above). Make two rows of machine gathering stitches along the seam line (i.e. 1 cm (⅜ in) in from the other edge). Draw up the gathering to the same length as the edge which is to be trimmed with the ruffle. Place the wrong side of the ruffle to the right side of the garment, raw edges together. Pin and tack in place. Finish with bias binding along the raw edge (see page 108).

BUTTONHOLES

To machine buttonholes, follow the directions in your machine manual.

BY HAND

Place a pin across each end of the buttonhole. Cut the buttonhole in the material with scissors. The pins will prevent you cutting too far by accident.

On the right side, make a row of tiny running stitches around the buttonhole, 2 mm (¹⁄₁₆ in) away from the raw edge. Next, without cutting off the thread, buttonhole stitch all round the slit, covering the running stitches.

When the ends are reached, make two or three straight stitches on top of one another at right angles to the slit before continuing with buttonhole stitch up the next side. Finish off on the wrong side by drawing the thread under a

few of the buttonhole stitches. Large buttonholes make a garment look very home-made, so choose only small buttons and sew the buttonholes with just a single strand of thread, using small stitches.

BUTTONS

Buttons may be sewn on using ordinary sewing thread or coloured embroidery silks. The easiest way to judge where to sew on the buttons, if it is not marked on the pattern is as follows:

Place the row of buttonholes over the material to be buttoned in the correct position. Through each buttonhole, catch a thread or two of the material with a pin. Leaving the pins in position, carefully slide the pins through the buttonholes, so that the buttonhole material can be lifted off. Sew buttons in the positions where the pins have remained.

It is always best to check the button positions are in the right place by this method even if the pattern does have the buttons marked.

Using a double strand of thread sew on the buttons with several straight stitches. Secure on the reverse side of the material.

DECORATIVE STITCHES FOR BUTTONS

FOUR-HOLED BUTTONS

Using three strands of embroidery silk in a

contrasting colour, sew through the buttons with vertically, horizontally or diagonally sewn straight stitches from hole to hole.

TWO-HOLED BUTTONS WITH STAR-SHAPED CUT-OUT

The holes in the button may be vertical or horizontal. Secure the button first in the normal manner with sewing thread.

Using three strands of embroidery silk, bring the thread up through the material and hole B from the reverse side. Take the thread down through hole A. Bring the thread up through hole B once again. Insert the point of the needle in a downwards direction under the sewing thread joining A to B. Wind the embroidery silk round the needle point three times and pull the needle through the sewing thread and the loops just made around it. Take the thread back down hole B. This makes one french knot.

Bring the needle up through hole A, insert the needle in an upwards direction under the sewing thread joining A to B. Wind the embroidery silk round the needle point three times and pull the needle through the sewing thread and the loops just made around it. Take the thread back down hole A. This makes the second french knot.

Fasten off securely.

As an alternative, the first knot may be made in a different colour from the second, fastening off on the reverse side between the two stages.

PRESS-STUDS

Press-studs are occasionally used to fasten edges which overlap, where there is not room to make a buttonhole.

Sew the knob half of the press-stud on the overlap edge. To place the other half of the stud, close the overlap and pass a needle through the overlap material, the centre of the knob section and down into the underneath material. Sew the centre of the other half of the stud where the needle is stuck.

Alternatively, press the knob half against the underneath material and it will leave a tiny dent showing where the other half is to be sewn.

EMBROIDERY

MACHINE EMBROIDERY

All the patterns for embroidery in this book are sewn by hand but it is easy for anyone who prefers machine embroidery to substitute her own designs.

As sewing machines vary from one make to another, it is not possible to give full instructions here. The manufacturer's booklet should give details and this information should be studied carefully before beginning to embroider on a garment.

TRANSFERRING EMBROIDERY MOTIF PATTERNS TO THE MATERIAL

Trace, copy or enlarge the embroidery design on to paper, using a black felt tip

POSITIONING A PRESS-STUD

111

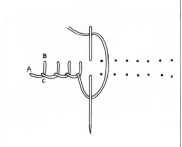

BUTTONHOLE STITCH

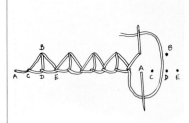

BLANKET STITCH

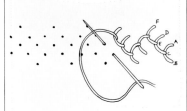

FEATHER STITCH

CHAIN STITCH

pen. Make sure this has dried, then, working near a light or window and on a flat surface, place the material over the drawing. Using a pencil, trace the design on to the material. When thick or dark-coloured materials are used, designs may be traced on to the surface of the material using dressmaker's carbon paper.

STITCHES
All the embroidery stitches should be worked using two strands of embroidery silk unless otherwise instructed.

BUTTONHOLE STITCH

Beginning at the left side, bring the needle and thread through to the front of the work at A. Insert the needle just above the line at B. With the needle pointing downwards, bring the point back through to the front at C. Let the thread fall under the point of the needle in a loop and draw through the thread. Repeat the procedure slightly to the right, but close to the stitch just made, until the line is complete.

BLANKET STITCH

Beginning at the left side, bring the needle and thread through at A. Insert the needle just above the line and slightly to the right at B. With the needle pointing downwards at a slight angle, bring the point back through to the front at C. Let the thread fall under the point of the needle in a loop and draw right through. Reinsert the needle at B and

bring the point through to the front at D, letting the thread fall under the needle. Draw through. Reinsert the needle at B once again and bring the point out at E, keeping the thread under the point. Draw through.

Repeat the stitch until the row is complete, E becomes C on the next stitch. Keep the stitches evenly spaced.

Both these stitches may be used to decorate an edge, for example round a collar or cuff, in which case keep the needle point downwards below the edge instead of bringing it through the material at C, D and E.

FEATHER STITCH

Bring the needle through at A. Keeping the thread to the left and under the needle, insert at B and bring it out at C. Insert the needle at D, slightly above and to the left of C. Bring it out again at E. Continue in this manner, keeping the thread under the needle. When F is reached, bring the stitches down again. Do not pull the loops tightly when bringing the needle through.

CHAIN STITCH

This can be made in straight lines or curves.
Come up at A, put the needle in again at A leaving a small loop. Come up again at B, just inside the loop. Draw the thread through but do not pull up too tightly. Go in again at B leaving a small loop and come up again at C, just inside the loop. Draw the thread through gently.

Repeat the stitch along the line or curve to be embroidered, beginning each stitch just inside the previous loop. Keep the loops an even length.

LAZY DAISY STITCH

Bring the needle through at A. Reinsert the needle at A and, holding the thread under the needle, bring the needle back through at B. Draw the thread through, pulling to form a small loop. Take the needle and thread through to the back at C.

OVERSTITCH

Keeping the thread above the needle, come up at A, go down at B, come up at C, go down at D and come up at E. Repeat down the line, keeping the stitch as small as possible by picking up only one or two threads of the material. Make each stitch as close to the previous one as possible.

STEM STITCH

Bring the needle up at A. Keeping the thread to the left and underneath the needle, take a stitch with the needle pointing upwards, inserting it at B and bringing it up at C. Draw the thread through. Continue until the line is completed.

SATIN STITCH

Satin stitch is made up of a series of straight stitches sewn side by side, so that no material can be seen between them. It is used to make shapes of small to medium size.

Bring the needle up from the wrong side on the left hand edge of the outline to be filled. Take it down again exactly opposite on the right hand edge of the outline. Bring the needle up on the left hand edge again as close to the start of the first stitch as possible. Carry on in this manner until the space is filled. Do not pull the stitches so tight that the material rucks.
This stitch is often worked slanting rather than horizontally across the outline and when it is done like this it gives a very shiny effect.

FRENCH KNOTS

French knots vary in size according to the number of twists and the thickness of the thread they are worked in. Three should be the maximum number of twists for a french knot here.
Bring the needle up from the wrong side. Take a tiny stitch, looping the thread to the left of the needle. Twist the thread the required number of times round the needle point. Reinsert the needle into the material as close to where it came up as possible, drawing the thread through the loops and the material. Instructions for working french knots on two-holed buttons are given under the button heading, page 111.

BULLION KNOTS

Bullion knots are very similar to french knots. They look very effective wrapped closely together to resemble rosebuds. Daisies are also easily made with this stitch.

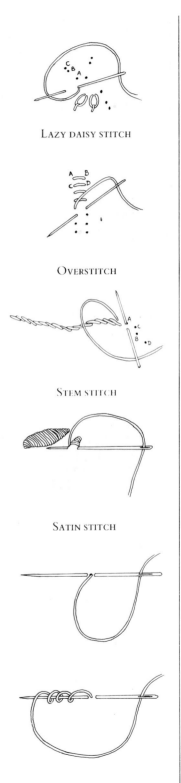

LAZY DAISY STITCH

OVERSTITCH

STEM STITCH

SATIN STITCH

MAKING A FRENCH KNOT

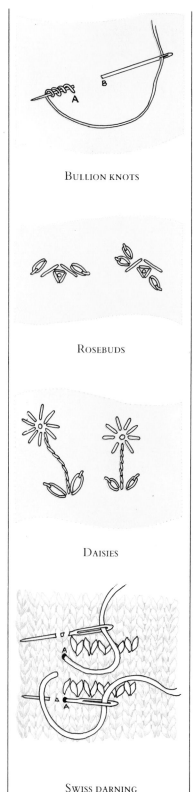

BULLION KNOTS

ROSEBUDS

DAISIES

Bring the needle up from the wrong side at A. Pick up a few threads of material to the right of A, inserting the point of the needle at B and bringing it up again at A. Do not pull the needle right through. Twist the thread round the needle point the required number of times (five or seven times for the projects in this book). Hold these loops down with the left thumb and pull the needle and thread through. Reinsert the needle at B and pull the thread through to the back. The twists should lie along the surface of the material between A and B.

ROSEBUDS WITH LEAVES

The rosebuds vary in size according to the thickness of the thread. They are best worked with two strands of embroidery silk on material and with three strands of embroidery silk on knitted garments. They may be made in one colour with green leaves but the best effect of all is achieved when a darker shade is used for the central french knot. Keep the stitches close together.

1. Make a three-twist french knot in the centre of where you wish the rosebud to be.
2. Stitch three five-twist bullion knots in a triangle round the french knot as shown.
3. Make two seven-twist bullion knots lying across the bottom corners of the triangle as shown.
4. Make lazy daisy stitches (see page 113) for the leaves.

DAISY

1. Make a three-twist french knot in yellow silk for the centre of the flower.
2. In white silk, stitch seven-twist bullion knots around the french knot as shown.
3. Using green silk, work stem stitch (see page 113) down the stalk and make two lazy daisy stitches (see page 113) at the bottom.

SWISS DARNING

Swiss darning is a counted stitch, worked over the top of a knitted stocking stitch background. It is usually worked in wool but embroidery silks may be used. The stitches may form a picture worked from a chart, or may be single stitches used to decorate a garment.

Any small cross stitch charted design may be used, providing there are sufficient stitches on the garment. One square on the chart represents one stitch. Bring the needle up at A, just below the stitch to be worked. Pass the needle underneath the bottom of the stitch above from right to left, bringing the thread with it. Insert the needle back down at A. Continue along the row working from right to left and completing one row before moving on to the next.

COUNTED THREAD WORK

An evenweave material should be used. One coloured square on the charts represents one cross stitch. Decide on the size of your cross stitch. On the evenweave used for the patterns in this book (i.e. with 26 threads to 2.5 cm/1 in) one hole is left free between A/C and B/C.

CROSS STITCH

Journey one:
Begin at A and make a diagonal stitch across to B. Bring the needle up at C and make another diagonal stitch to D. Continue along the row in this direction until the next colour is reached, finishing at the lower point of the stitch.

Journey two:
Make the return journey crossing the diagonal stitch already made with another, going in and out of the same holes, forming a cross. Work from A across to B and down to C and so on until the start is reached.

BACK STITCH

Back stitch, which is used to outline cross stitch patterns, should be worked after the cross stitch is finished. Each stitch should be the same length as one cross stitch.

Begin at one end of the line to be backstitched. Make a row of running stitches going in and out according to the chart. When the end is reached, make a return journey, this time filling in the gaps.

WITHDRAWN THREAD WORK

LADDER HEM STITCH

The stitch used in this book is worked on the right side of the material. Use one strand of embroidery silk, or a single strand of coloured sewing cotton to work

the stitch.

1. Draw out one thread from the material down the centre of the area to be embroidered. Draw out two more threads on both sides of this gap, making a total of five drawn threads.

2. Turn the work, so that the gap made by the withdrawn threads is horizontal.

3. Secure the cotton at the left side of the work on the reverse. Bring the needle through the material to the front at A, i.e. at the beginning of the bottom edge and two horizontal threads below. Take the needle past five vertical threads to the right. Pass the needle between threads 5 and 6, at B. Bring the needle round the back and pass to the front again through the vertical threads at C. Inserting the needle between the vertical threads at B again and pointing it downwards, bring the point up through the material two horizontal threads below at D. Pull the cotton fairly tight, so that the five vertical threads enclosed are pulled into a small bundle. Repeat the stitch until the side is complete. Fasten off.

4. Turn the work upside down to stitch the other edge of the drawn thread gap. Work in the same manner as step 3, taking care that the needle is passed between the same vertical threads as on the previous side. The threads will then be pulled into ladder-like bundles.

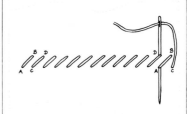

CROSS STITCH: BEGINNING
JOURNEY 2

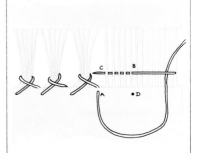

LADDER HEM STITCH

SCOLLOPS: ACTUAL SIZE

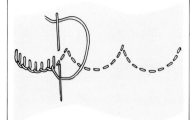

SCOLLOP STITCHING

SCOLLOPING

This embroidery stitch gives a firm decorative finish to raw edges, so that they do not fray. The scollops may be any size; the small size suitable for babies' and children's garments is given here.
Use two strands of embroidery silk for a fine scollop.
1. Using a pencil, trace the scollops along the seam line (1 cm (³⁄₈ in) from the edge of the material), so that the curves of the scollops fall into the seam allowance.
2. Work three to four scollops at a time. Begin by making tiny running stitches (see page 106) from right to left along the scollops just drawn.
3. Work tiny, closed buttonhole stitches (see page 112) back along the running stitches. The purled edge of the buttonhole stitch should cover the running stitches round the curves.
Keep the stitches vertical throughout, do not slope the stitches into the curves.
4. When the row is completed, cut away the material as close to the buttonhole edge as possible, taking care not to snip the stitches.

SMOCKING

Smocking is a special favourite for children's clothes, as it has a great deal of elasticity and the garments, therefore, stretch readily as a child grows. Although making the gathers is the most laborious part of the process, it should be done carefully and unhurriedly, since it is the most important part and uneven gathers can never be successfully straightened later. The smocking is always done before the garment is made.
It is not easy to give a definite guide to the amount of material needed, as thin materials require more than thicker ones. The spacing between the dots also affects the amount of material needed but a rough guide is three times the finished width of the piece the smocking is to be applied to. The amount of material allowed in the patterns is sufficient for most materials suitable for children's clothes.

APPLYING THE DOTS

The spacing needed for all the smocking in this book is 5 mm (¼ in) across and 5 mm (¼ in) down. This is the best spacing for any smocking on delicate articles or children's clothes and gives the most professional-looking result. The number of rows needed are given for each garment, or if using another smocking design, the number will be indicated in the instructions. There are various methods of applying dots and gathering the material. One is to buy sheets of transfer dots from embroidery shops or good department stores but they are not successful on most materials used to make children's clothes. Despite their claims, they do not wash out and can be seen through the material from the right side.
Another method is to use a

pleater machine, which will gather the material ready for the embroidery, however, although this is very useful when doing a lot of smocking, there is no substitute for gathering the material by hand.

The best method for the patterns in this book is as follows:

Mark the dots, at the intervals required, on to tissue paper using a ruler and pencil. Take care that they are exact. (It is possible, with care, to iron dot transfers on to the tissue paper.) Pin the tissue paper securely to the wrong side of the material, aligning the first row of dots no more than 3 mm (⅛ in) below the seam line. Alternatively, mark the dots with a pencil directly on to the wrong side of the material.

GATHERING THE SMOCKING

Each row is gathered with a separate thread, long enough to complete an entire row in one piece. As these gathering threads are also used as a guide for the embroidery stitches, contrasting thread may be used on dark materials. It is best to stick to white thread on lighter material, because occasionally coloured thread will stain a fine material when withdrawn.

Make a good knot in the end of each thread. On the wrong side of the material, run the needle from dot to dot, in a row, picking up each one with a tiny stitch through both the material and the tissue paper. Repeat down the entire depth

of the smocking before gathering the threads. Tear the tissue paper away.

When all the rows are stitched, pull the threads evenly until the gathered material is slightly narrower than the width required. Do not cut off the surplus thread but hold it fast by winding in a figure-of-eight round pins placed upright at the end of the rows. Threads may be divided into three per pin.

Spread the gathers evenly across the fullness.

BASIC STITCHES

Most of the basic stitches used in smocking come from the same stitch; it is just the placing and combination of this stitch that gives rise to the more intricate patterns. It is a good idea to practise these stitches on scraps of gathered material before attempting the garments in the book if you have not done any smocking before.

When gathering and smocking the long pieces, it is easiest to work the design so that each row begins immediately beneath the one above, down the depth of the panel. This is the oldest way of working smocking in a garment. The more experienced smocker will be able to work the smocking designs round the armholes, as has been done on the clothes in the photographs. Any smocking design can be used on the patterns in this book, providing the number of rows in the panel does not go down lower than the waist line on the garment.

SMOCKING DOTS: ACTUAL SIZE

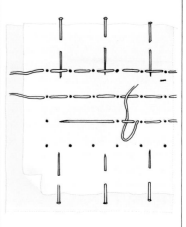

PICKING UP DOTS

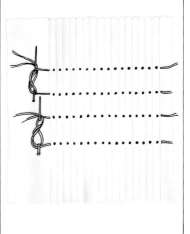

PULLING UP GATHERS

The smocking is embroidered on the right side of the material and normally with two or three strands of embroidery thread. It is worked from left to right, the needle held horizontally and picking up one gather to the right each time. The needle is always inserted into the gather from right to left. The stitches should be pulled, so that they are not so tight that the gather is pulled out of place, but also not too loose, as this would cause the smocked panel to stretch too much.

The threads that have been used to gather the material on the wrong side become guide threads for the smocking design when viewed from the right side.

NB The numbered rows in the pattern designs refer to the guide threads and not to the rows of embroidery.

Each row is ended by inserting the needle back into the last gather and catching it on the reverse side two or three times.

When the whole panel has been worked, the pins are removed and the guide threads pulled carefully out.

OUTLINE STITCH

This is one of the best stitches to use for the top row of smocking as it controls the gathers.

Beginning at the extreme left of the work, make a knot and bring the needle and thread through the first gather from the wrong side, at the same height as the guide thread. Pick up a few threads from each gather, letting the thread fall underneath the needle each time.

Continue along the row in this manner.

CABLE STITCH

This stitch also controls the gathers and so is useful for the top line. It is the one I usually choose, because the first row is difficult to embroider evenly, and cable stitch hides this better than outline stitch.

Make a knot and bring the needle and thread through the first gather at the same height as the guide thread. Pick up a few threads from the next gather to the right, keeping the thread above the needle. Still at the same height, pick up a few threads from the next pleat, this time letting the thread fall underneath the needle.

Continue in this manner, alternately keeping the thread above and below the needle.

DIAMOND STITCH

This stitch is an extension of cable stitch.

1. Bring the needle through the first gather at the same height as guide thread 1. Make a stitch to the right, picking up a few threads from the next gather, still at the same height and keeping the thread above the needle.

2. Bring the needle down to the level of guide thread 2 and make a stitch through the second gather, keeping the thread above the needle.

3. On the third gather, make a stitch at the same height as guide thread 2 but this time keeping the thread below the needle.

4. Take the needle back up to guide thread 1 on the fourth gather and make a stitch keeping the thread down. Repeat this procedure across the smocking panel. When two or more rows of this stitch are made in opposite directions, diamonds are formed (see figure A).

WAVE STITCH

1. Bring the needle through the first gather at the same height as guide thread 1. Make a stitch to the right, picking up a few threads from the next gather, still at the same height and keeping the thread above the needle.

2. Take the needle half way down towards guide thread 2 and make a stitch through the second gather, again keeping the thread above the needle.

3. Take the needle completely down to guide thread 2 on the third gather and make a stitch, keeping the thread above the needle.

4. On the fourth gather make a stitch at the same height as guide thread 2 but this time dropping the thread below the needle.

5. For the fifth gather take the needle half way up to guide thread 1, keeping the thread below the needle.

6. Take the needle right up to guide thread 1 on the sixth gather, still keeping the thread down. Repeat this procedure across the smocking panel until the row is complete. When two or three rows of wave stitch are made a chevron is formed (see

figure B).

These are the basic stitches used to form the designs in this book. Many variations can be made, for example, wave stitch may have several stitches between the top and bottom one. Designs are also varied by working following rows in the same direction or as a mirror image.

BULLION KNOTS AND ROSEBUDS

Bullion knots, rosebuds and leaves are worked on the smocking in the same way as described in the embroidery section on pages 113–14. Bullion and french knots are usually worked over two gathers.

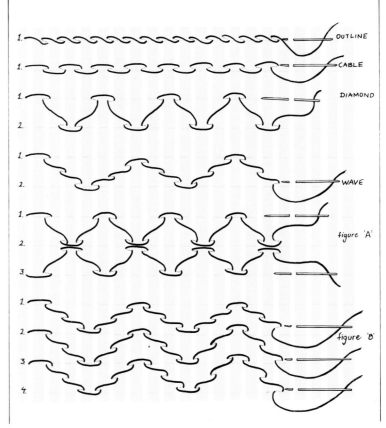

1.   OUTLINE

1.   CABLE

1.   DIAMOND

2.

1.

2.   WAVE

1.

2.   figure 'A'

3.

1.

2.   figure 'B'

3.

4.

GENERAL INFORMATION

ALTERING FOR GROWTH

HEMS

Hems are an obvious place to allow room for growth. A good double hem of 5 to 8 cm (2 or 3 in) will give several years' growth, as well as adding a touch of luxury to the garment.

The first time it is let down it should be rehemmed with a single hem to the fold line and this will hide the crease that often remains. The next time, it should be let down completely and rehemmed with seam binding.

Do use seam binding rather than just making do with a narrow hem, as the width of the binding looks like a hem and it also gives weight to the skirt, making the dress hang well.

To use seam binding:
The binding should be approximately 5 cm (2 in) wide and of the same colour as the dress. Stitch one edge to the bottom of the hem edge. Turn in the binding along the line just stitched and sew to the skirt with a slipstitch (see page 105).

TUCKS

Tucks on skirts or dresses provide a substantial amount of material to let down.

The tucks are just unpicked in the normal manner when the skirt needs lengthening. Wash the garment after the tuck has been unpicked, then iron the crease well.

BUTTONS

Growth room may be allowed in boys' romper suits by making the suit with an extra-wide underbuttonband. The buttons can then be moved towards the edge as the baby grows.

Buster suits can be lengthened simply by repositioning the buttons which hold the trousers on to the shirt.

It is not necessary to allow much room for an increase in width as children do not alter so much in this direction. The garment is often discarded before it is too tight across the chest. One thing which may be useful is to sew a 2.5 cm (1 in) buttonband to the button edge of the dress or romper, so that the buttons can be repositioned, allowing a little more room across the back.

Buttonband:
Cut a piece of the material chosen for the garment 6 cm (2½ in) wide and 1 cm (⅜ in) longer than the button edge. Fold the strip in half lengthways, wrong sides together, and press. With the right side of the strip to the right side of the button edge, stitch together with a plain seam 6 mm (¼ in) from the raw edges. Fold the strip in half, along the line pressed, to the other side. Turn in 6 mm (¼ in) seam allowance and slipstitch to the stitching line. Tuck in the raw edges at the top and bottom and slipstitch closed. The buttons are sewn on in the normal positions and

gradually let out as the child grows.

TO CONVERT A DRESS INTO A ROMPER

It is quite easy to convert a dress into a romper using the following instructions but thought should be given to the fact that it is not often possible to turn it back into a dress again. In some cases it may be preferable to leave the dress as it is for future generations and make a completely new romper.

1. Carefully let down the hem of the dress, then press the crease out with an iron.
2. Measure the length from the centre neck to the centre front of the hem and mark the skirt at 39.5 cm (15½ in) for age 6 months or 44 cm (17¼ in) for age 1 year. Cut the skirt to this length.
3. Make a narrow 8 mm (⁵⁄₁₆ in) casing along the bottom edge, leaving 7.5 cm (3 in) free at the centre front and back.
4. Thread 20 cm (8 in) elastic (adjust here if necessary to the size of the baby's leg plus 2 cm/¾ in) through the leg casings and secure with several small stitches.
5. Returning to the centre front and back, make a narrow hem the same size as the leg casing and slipstitch in place.
6. Make two buttonholes on the front hem between the leg casings. Sew two buttons in corresponding places on the back hem.

CHOOSING THE RIGHT MATERIALS

It is amazing how easy it is to make a very nice garment look home-made by using large stitches and buttons, bulky bindings and nylon ribbons. Dressmaking should not be a cheap way of making poor clothes and with a little care and attention this can be avoided.

Read all instructions carefully before beginning, have everything to hand and give yourself plenty of time.

SCISSORS

Sharp-pointed scissors are a great aid to sewing and it is worthwhile investing in one of the more expensive makes.

NEEDLES

Large stitches soon make a garment look very home-made and topstitching is often neglected, which is a pity, because it gives a very professional look to a garment. Many people think that it takes experience to make tiny neat stitches and are surprised to find the cause of clumsy stitches is usually that too large a needle is being used. Crewel needles are normally used for embroidery but the size 10 crewel needle is recommended here for all sewing.

A size 60/70 (8/10) machine needle should be used on the fine materials chosen for these patterns.

A darning needle with a large eye is needed for sewing knitted pieces together and a small tapestry needle for the counted cross stitch work. Bodkins (large, thick, blunt needles with wide eyes) are the best type to use for threading ribbons through eyelets.

PINS

Dressmaker's pins are normally used in the working of these garments but if the material is very fine, they may leave holes when removed. To avoid this, use fine sewing needles to pin the pieces together.

THREADS

Sewing thread should be chosen to match the material used. If cotton thread is used on polyester materials it causes puckering, because the thread shrinks when washed while the polyester material doesn't. Threads come in various thicknesses, the two most common being 40 and 50. Normally the higher the number, the finer the thread, so do look around and buy the thinnest thread you can find. If the thread keeps knotting, it is probably being threaded the wrong way. Try threading the needle before cutting the thread off the reel, putting the knot at the cut-off end.

MATERIALS

Natural materials, such as wool and cotton, remain firm favourites for children but now mixtures of man-made and natural fibres provide easy-care materials. Viyella (55% wool; 45% cotton) and Clydella (80% cotton; 20% wool) have been traditionally associated with children's clothes. They are hard-wearing and hang well. It is also possible to buy materials of a similar mixture under other brand names, alternatively flannelette is of a suitable weight. Viyella, Clydella or flannelette are used in the winter and at night time for warmth. Babies usually need this even in the summer at night, when it is still quite chilly. For daytime in summer, cotton batiste and lawn are a good choice but polyester cottons are an easy-care alternative. Avoid 100% nylon materials as they are too hot for young children. Whatever mixture is chosen, select plain colours or classic patterns, such as checks, spots and small, simple designs – gaudy prints soon date. Another source of material is cast-off adult clothing. Needlecord and corduroy skirts are very useful for buster-suit shorts, while dresses and full skirts often have sufficient material in them to make a small smocked dress for a girl. Beware of large prints though, as they do not become young children.

WOOLS

Knitting wools are available in pure wool, Courtelle/wool or Courtelle/nylon mixtures. Pure wool is soft and a more natural colour but does require careful laundering. The Courtelle/nylon mixtures are more useful, except for special occasions, but take the time to sort out the wools with the least amount of nylon in them, as wool with a high proportion of nylon in it makes a garment look cheap when knitted up. Again, avoid any 100% nylon wool, since babies soon become overheated when dressed in this.

Choose 2 and 3 plys for indoor clothing; thick wools so easily look bulky on young children, which is disappointing after all the work put into making the garments.

TRIMMINGS

Edgings, insertion and beading are all available in broderie anglaise, nylon and cotton lace. The decision about which to use should be governed by the material it is to be sewn to. Wool mixture materials require cotton lace, while polyester materials need nylon lace.

Colour, too, has to be taken into consideration, sometimes an apparently white background to a print is really off-white, then cotton lace is called for, as it, too, tends to be off-white. Broderie anglaise may be used on cottons or white Viyella. If a coloured lace or anglaise is wanted, it is best to dye it at home, as bought coloured trimmings are usually too garish to use.

Trimmings on a garment should be consistent, for example, if a garment has a broderie anglaise waistband, then broderie anglaise, rather than lace, should also be chosen to edge the neckline and sleeve bands.

Cotton and nylon laces are quite widely available, though

it is best to choose the more delicate varieties of nylon lace, as some heavier ones do make the finished garment look home-made. Surprisingly, it is not always the more expensive ones that are the best, very fine ones can be bought in the lower price ranges.

There are three types of trimming and there is much confusion between them: Edging has one decorative edge and one unfinished edge. It may be used straight, or gathered before stitching to the garment. Edging may also be bought ready gathered and bound but this gives a very bulky binding and should be avoided.

Insertion has two straight finished edges and is used between two pieces of material.

Eyelet insertion, also known as beading, is the same as insertion but has holes at intervals along it to thread ribbons through.

RIBBONS

Satin, rather than nylon, ribbons should be chosen, as their shiny texture lends a luxurious effect to the finished garment. Satin ribbon comes in single or double-sided versions and the choice of colours and shades is immense. Single-sided ribbon is useful for slotting through, for example, eyelet insertion, but if the ribbon is to be tied, then double-sided ribbon is better as a wrong side will not show.

TYING A BOW

When tying a small bow with single-sided ribbon, follow these steps (the shiny satin side is the right side of the ribbon):

1. Fold a small loop, wrong sides together (approximately 2 cm (¾ in) from the beginning of the ribbon for a small bow).

2. Holding the loop between the fingers of the right hand, take the longer end of the ribbon and, twisting it wrong side up, wrap loosely round the loop from the bottom front to the bottom back.

3. With wrong sides together, push another small loop through the back of the middle wrap and pull tight.

4. Cut the ribbon ends to a point.

If these steps are followed, the two loops of the bow and one tie will have the shiny side of the satin showing.

If tying two ribbons together in a bow, for example on the waistband of the newborn nightgown, tie the two ribbons together with a knot first. Next turn the article upside down and follow steps 1 to 4, making step 1 near the knot. This ensures that the long ties fall nicely downwards when turned right way up.

The centre of the bow may be decorated with a tiny material flowerhead or a minute pearl bead ring. These can be bought from the larger haberdasheries.

GARMENT CARE

After all the work that has gone into making the garments, it is worth putting a little effort into the laundering of them.

WASHING

Most garments do stay newer-looking if they are hand-washed. This is not as troublesome as it sounds if it is done each day, before the garments really have time to get dirty. A good compromise is to wash them by hand, popping them into the machine occasionally to spruce them up.

All the garments in this book, unless knitted in pure wool, can be washed in the normal way on a minimum-iron washing machine programme. Biological washing powders should not be used, as they often cause rashes, particularly on babies' delicate skins. Stergene or similar is recommended for hand-washing. Knitted garments should be pulled into shape after washing and laid out flat to dry.

When white baby clothes are beginning to turn grey, they can soon be brought back to life by soaking overnight in Fairy Snow, following the instructions on the packet. Clothes that have been kept from previous generations and have become yellowed may also be soaked in this way without coming to any harm and, when rinsed out, will be brilliant white once again.

IRONING

Articles knitted in pure wool will need ironing with a damp cloth between the knitting and the iron.

It is important that wool mixtures are never ironed, as this distorts the shape and flattens any pattern.

Smocking, also, should never be ironed, as this would flatten the pleats, but all other dressmaking and embroidery is vastly improved by ironing. Embroidery should be ironed on the wrong side. The embroidery stitches then sink into the ironing board cover giving a lovely raised effect when ironed.

STORAGE

It is lovely to receive clothes that have been kept and handed down from previous generations, especially if they were worn by you as a child. At the very least it is worth keeping baby clothes for the next infant. What child has not heard the words 'You used to wear that when you were a baby!' with fascination?

Garments should never be put away dirty but washed and thoroughly dried before storing. They should be laid flat, using lots of tissue paper to prevent creases and be kept in the dark. Do not hang clothes to store them, because this distorts the seams.

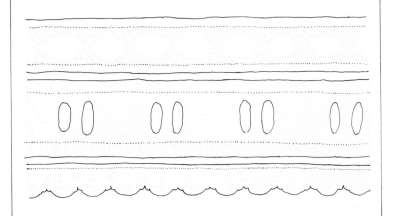

TRIMMINGS – TOP: INSERTION; MIDDLE: EYELET INSERTION; BOTTOM: EDGING

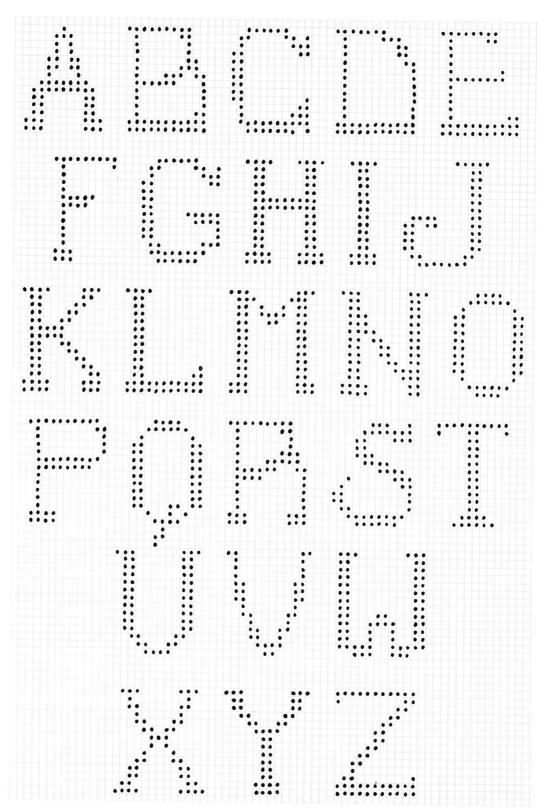

CROSS STITCH ALPHABET

INDEX
(Figures in italics refer to photographs)

ABCDE
FGHIJ
KLMNO
PQRST
UVWX
XYZ